BARON LIONAL NATHAN DE ROTHSCHILD.

Member of Parliament, for the City of London.

RUNNING SKETCHES

OF

Men and Places,

IN

ENGLAND, FRANCE, GERMANY, BELGIUM,
AND SCOTLAND.

BY

GEORGE COPWAY,
(KAH-GE-GA-GAH-BOWH)
CHIEF OF THE OJIBWAY NATION, NORTH AMERICAN INDIANS.

With Illustrations.

NEW YORK:
J. C. RIKER, 129 FULTON STREET.
1851.

Entered according to Act of Congress, in the year 1851, by
GEORGE COPWAY,
In the Clerk's Office for the Southern District of New York.

STEREOTYPED BY THOMAS B. SMITH,
216 WILLIAM STREET, N. Y.

TO

RICHARD PENNELL, M.D.,

AND HIS LADY,

AS A MARK OF THE HIGHEST RESPECT

AND GRATITUDE FOR THEIR KINDNESS,

This Volume

IS MOST RESPECTFULLY DEDICATED

BY THE AUTHOR.

Preface.

In putting out the following pages, it has been in part to satisfy the inquiries by my friends in this country, how I liked my tour through Europe, as well as to preserve the pleasing incidents which were shown me, by the people wherever I sojourned.

Without following the general course of travellers in encumbering their books in deep historical researches of the various countries they have visited,—I have merely put enough to interest the general reader, of the towns, and time-worn ruins which came under my personal observation.

Much of this is devoted to sketches of men now prominent before the European public, which I hope will repay the reader for the time occupied in reading them.

Evening after evening I have been requested to recite my impressions of the country since I have returned. I send forth this volume to the fireside of the paleface. All defects which may be found, (and they are numerous) I hope will be overlooked by them.

Now I am once more in the land of my fathers. A land dear to me; I love it better than ever,—and may the Great Spirit ever smile on the land of my birth.

Farewell

until you hear from me again—

KAH-GE-GA-GAH-BOWH.

NEW YORK, May, 1851.

CONTENTS.

CHAPTER VIII.

CHAPTER IX.

CHAPTER X.

CHAPTER XI.

CHAPTER XII.

CHAPTER XIII.

CHAPTER XIV.

CHAPTER XV.

CHAPTER XVI.

CHAPTER XVII.

CHAPTER XVIII.

CHAPTER XIX.

CHAPTER XX.

CHAPTER XXI.

CHAPTER XXII.

CHAPTER XXIII.

EUROPEAN OBSERVATIONS.

CHAPTER I.

THE DEPARTURE.

It is nearly five months since I first had any idea of going to Germany. It was suggested in a conversation I had with the great Philanthropist and celebrated "Learned Blacksmith," Elihu Burrett, in Washington. The fact of leaving my native land seems now a reality. The suggestions which were then made as a means of preparation, have been attended to—and now I am going to a country where the people will be strangers to me, and whose language will be different from mine—whose habits and manners will be altogether their own.

I have thought that I loved my native land; but I realize it more to-day than ever; and all that is lovely in my native land is magnified. I can see at this moment all the scenes of beauty and grandeur which I have beheld in the forest world. The rivers whose courses I have traced as they glided in deep shadow through the forests—the beautiful lakes on whose wooded banks I have wandered in childhood—are rising in my view ; and alternately pleasure and regret flit across my breast as I think of the varied past.

Valley after valley, and mountain after mountain appears in view, and in each I recognize a familiar face, which often greeted me in the land where I first drew my breath, and found I had my life in a world of toil. I may see other countries equally beautiful and grand in scenery, yet let me be an enthusiast for my own dear native land. To-day the power of steam and the arms of iron must sever me from my friends and country. My path no one knows save the Deity ! The waste of waters and their eternal war !—what will be my sensations when I shall first see the *Old World?* What kind of country is England ? is Germany ?

Such were my thoughts while seated in the Adams House, in Boston, to take my breakfast for the last time before sailing—and while musing thus, I perceived quite a commotion among the boarders as they sat at table, and I could distinguish the following sad sentences, "The President is dead! He died last evening." Then General Zachariah Taylor is no more! and we shall take to Europe the news of his death. My only wish on hearing of this event was for his safety; and I hoped the Great Spirit had forgiven him for killing so many of the red men of my country.

"Haste! Haste!" the hands of my watch told me, as I found that the time of my departure was near. Everything being in readiness, I took to the steamer, where I met my friends.

What a beautiful morning! The sky so clear, and brought nearer, as it were, by sympathy with earth! The air, heated by the warm sun, came to us soft and balmy, as our vessel lay anchored in the shade. Life in the crowded streets, and noise of carts echoing in the business part of the city; and Commerce pouring her treasures from every clime to the wharf of Boston! Having gazed with wonder and admiration on the ships, and wharves, and warehouses, I stepped on board the beautiful Niagara. I found one on board who is going to the Peace Congress, the Rev. Dr. Barrett, of Boston. He was attended by a band of soldiers, who honored him with their coming down to see him off, because he had tickled their ears with a very neat and appropriate sermon yesterday. Just five minutes before twelve o'clock, brandy, wine, and music. The Captain mounted the paddle-box, and called out "Let go!" and as the wheels moved, I mounted the long-boat and delivered the following address to my friends on the wharf: which having delivered, I had to throw at them.

"The day is bright'ning which we long have sought,
I see its early light and hail its dawn:
The gentle voice of Peace my ear hath caught,
And from my forest home I greet the morn.
Here, now, I meet you with a brother's hand—
Bid you farewell—then speed me on my way
To join the white men in a foreign land,
And from the dawn bring on the bright noonday.
Noonday of Peace! O, glorious jubilee,
When all mankind are one from sea to sea.

Farewell, my native land, rock, hill, and plain,
River and lake, and forest home adieu;
Months shall depart e'er I shall tread again
Amid your scenes, and be once more with you.
I leave thee now; but wheresoe'er I go,
Whatever scenes of grandeur meet my eyes,

My heart can but ONE native country know,
And that, the fairest land beneath the skies.
America! farewell; thou art that gem,
Brightest and fairest in earth's diadem."

Having backed to the middle of the stream, our wheels rolled and thundered forward, and with the first revolutions they made, our iron lungs went

"*Bang,*" "*Bang.*"

The echo having died away, we were soon seen in the distance.

The harbor of Boston appears most to advantage when looking at it from the water. The waters are still, and yet the surface is all life-crafts of every name and size, and vessels from every country! The flags of nations here wave without fear.

The further we were borne on by our ship, the more the city of Boston seemed to lift up her spires, glittering before the sun. The State House rising above the rest, appeared to look down the chimneys around it. Viewing this I thought of my first excursion to its summit, eleven years ago, when I first attempted to learn the ways and language of the Pale Face. From yonder steeple I then gazed with wonder and astonishment on the works of the white man. I had just come from the forest, where the white man with his axe had hardly ever entered. Tracing my varied life was like watching the snow-white clouds, which though lovely, now assume a dark and frowning aspect, and anon, when they have been rent by storms, are light and fleecy.

As we ploughed down and out of the harbor, the sea seemed ready to fold us in its arms. A lovelier day I have hardly ever seen. May the Gods be kind and propitious!

The last thing I could see in the distance was the Bunker Hill Monument, which appeared to tower over all the surrounding country. This column was reared in commemoration of a battle, and in honor of men who fought bravely for their firesides, while they expelled the red man from his native soil. The day I hope is not far distant when the cause of Humanity will be blessed with the men who will change this spirit of hero-worship into adoration for everything noble and elevating. Then shall columns devoted to the Prince of Peace arise one after another to the clouds, which shall be like beacon lights in the highway of Progress for the generations yet to come.

The rocky Islands loomed far off in our view, and soon nothing but the dark outline of the land could be seen—and still I gazed and gazed, and when it had become concealed from sight, I could with a heart full of affection for my native land, say—

> "America, America! Heaven's blessing attend her!
> While we live we will cherish, and love, and defend her.
> Tho' the scorner may sneer at, and witlings defame her,
> Our hearts swell with gladness whenever we name her."

To the following gentlemen I am greatly indebted for their kindness in preparing for my journey. God bless them. I have never asked a true American anything but I have received. I can do nothing more than to love and cherish them. Their smiles have left a lasting sensation in my heart. I may find in the world men equally kind to me, but these I shall never forget: J. P. Bigelow, the Mayor, Amos Lawrence, Julius A. Palmer, and Mr. Walworth.

I might name others who have been my friends in Boston. Those have upheld me in all my efforts—they gave me encouragement in their expression of good-will to my race, and notwithstanding all the many aggravated wrongs which my poor brethren have received from the hands of the Pale Face. I have a nature within me which, when I see the kind acts of the white man, covers a multitude of sins.

I have regarded the Christian of this country as one whose opportunities of doing good have been numerous; and who when he has embraced these opportunities has enjoyed more of Heaven's smiles than any one could experience elsewhere.

On board this Steamer bound for Europe are people from all parts of the United States—from the south, north and west—each having an object in view. Some are going to the continent, and others on business of an official character, while others are in pursuit of happiness or riches. Here I am too—a Delegate to the Peace Congress in behalf of the *Christian Indians of America!* A few years, and what a change! Not very long ago I heard the war-cry of the West ringing in my ear. The scattered and mangled remains of noble figures I have seen! But the dawn of a better day has come. The war-whoop has died away in the song of praise to the Great Spirit. Art, Science, Literature, like a thousand streams, roll on their mighty tide, to purify and refine the Indian mind.

There is a man on board who seldom speaks—silent, thoughtful, grave, even to sadness. Who can he be? An Englishman in appearance: an Englishman I find him to be. But sad his experience! The Queen City of the West will be to him an interesting spot, for in travelling while there a bright and noble youth died, and that man is his father, carrying the sad intelligence to his own domestic circle of the death of his son. His intention was to have travelled all over the United States and the Canadas, that this son of his might see as much as was desirable of the New World before he should settle down in some professional calling.

But what a contrast! There is a Southern gentleman whose very finger ends are full of life, and whose witticisms set the whole company in a roar of laughter. So full of animation, so full of oddity is he that you have only to look that way and a hearty laugh will instantly put to flight a legion of "blues," if you happen to be troubled with these unwelcome visitors.

Sea-sickness! O what utter wretchedness and misery! The wind is fair, the sky is clear, and the boat moving at the rate of thirteen knots an hour. A table groaning with good things, but the very sight of them distracts you. I have been trying my best to eat, but cannot—and perfectly disgusted with the eatables of the saloon, good as they are, bid adieu to all, and "turn in" for the night about 8 o'clock.

CHAPTER II.

THE OCEAN.

Old Ocean! Here it is, surrounding me on all sides! —To the limit of human vision this expanse of waters is illimitable, except that it is bounded by the horizon, which forever recedes as we approach it. How appallingly is the mind impressed in contemplating these huge domains! What wonders lie in the world beneath—familiar to the monsters of the deep, but strange and mysterious to us. Here too are objects of terror—shoals and quicksands that lie treacherously concealed, waiting the behests of Fate, and the maniac fury of the Ocean to give to their desolate bosoms the treasures of which they are forever bereft. Our noble ship is now sailing over deep valleys and lofty mountains, like an eagle in upper air, and the peering eye of Imagination, which is sharper than the eagle's, sees far down, dismal caverns and the pavement of human bones. Perchance there are in that fathomless region those who perform the rites of Christian burial for the poor sailor, and that his body reposes in some sepulchre—but ah ! it cannot be.

A life on the sea and a life on the land—how striking the contrast ! Reverting from the present to my childhood, and from the sea to my home in the forest, I remember a sailor, by the name of Lewis, who strayed from the coast to my father's lodge, and who became so attached to our mode of life that he lived with us three or four years. When he came to understand our language so as to be understood in the wigwam, he told us many a thrilling tale of the sea. From this stray son of the ocean I gathered my reverence for the sea ; and the thought of its waves throbbing upon the shore swelled my heart with emotion. The one thought that has been with me ever since is of its awful grandeur, and of its sublime display of the Manitou who made all things.

This Lewis used to tell us of a monstrous great fish, no doubt the whale—and of sharks, sea-bears and mermaids. Such superstitious tales of the sea found a ready welcome in the wigwam of the Indian, by his warm fire and hospitable board. In the winter nights, eighteen years ago, I would sit with my chin resting on the palms of my hands, and, listening to Lewis, drink in the whole story of the ocean. His "yarns" were long and tough, hard to digest, yet I believed all he said, for his sage pipe, added to my veneration for age (for his locks were white and he had trod for years the hard path of experience), gave me the most implicit confidence in him. These tales, wakened to life by the sea-breeze, are now crowding in my head—but where is the sea-monster? Stop! be patient! we shall see the father of black fish by-and-by.

The second day out. No wind of any account—the sky is clear—the sun's heating rays pour on our deck—deep waves roll onward and before us, as if they feared to be overtaken—our foaming track stretches like a furrow over the field of waters—Our vessel rolls heavily onward, the arms of iron clashing below the deck, and the wheels thundering their revolutions through the foaming billows—Our bow now rising and bowing majestically, and now see-sawing over the ridge of a mountain wave. O delightful ride, were it not for sea-sickness! What indescribable misery does this single word impart! It is as if a dozen live chickens were fighting in you, or dancing a half-civilized polka. Imagine this, and you will have a good idea of sea-sickness. But enough of this, for it is now comparatively calm, and our company one by one ascend the quarter-deck to promenade with zigzag steps.

"A whale on the starboard side!" sang out one of the crew. There, sure enough, at more than two miles, distance, the spray rose at intervals, and long did I watch it, and not till it had passed from sight did I begin to realize that I was on the ocean, where there are monsters that play with the waves as if they were the ripples of a lake. Then again Lewis's "sea yarns" came trooping around me, and the sight I had just beheld gave fresh coloring to his pictures.

The fourth day. Still the wind is fair; our sails in full stretch—the waves rise higher and higher—a monotonous life in a very small kingdom is that on shipboard—yet we have here the Scotchman's "war-whoop," the bagpipe, squeaking most delightful music. The young man himself who greased the wheels of Time by opening and shutting his arms over the bag of wind, apparently enjoyed the sound: and certainly those who can find something to admire in this, have more discrimination than I am possessed of. Up and down he trod the quarter-deck, treading out his music and smiling at his fine performance—ogling and squinting, and laughing expressively at one corner of his mouth. This is what our backwoodsmen would call a big-horned music. But it is a good music when nothing else can be got; and thankful we are to enjoy it.

It is night again, and the bright-eyed stars one by one peer out, beholding themselves reflected in the sea. I stand on the stern of the boat, and whole worlds mirror their bright faces on this ocean. There goes a shooting star!—and along its fiery track lies a trail of glory, dying behind it. It is gone! but where? Why did the never-dying stars tremble as it passed?

I was taught in the woods that these bright stars were the homes of the good and the great—that each one was a representative of some hero of former ages, whose virtues shone in the skies according as he had done on earth. If so—which of these represent a Howard, a Raikes, a Calvin, a Luther, a Wesley, and a Washington? In deeds of virtue God is the *Sun*, and others appear, only when He is the centre of attraction. The sun has gone down in the west, carrying comets in his fiery bosom, but in a few short hours he will ascend the eastern skies, and glory will spread over the sea, and the rolling billows will shout his welcome. What a journey will the earth have accomplished in a few short hours!

But what is this compared with the speed of the *mind?* Give lightning the start by a million of furlongs, and the mind will be the first to reach its destination. It is itself a universe of stars, and of these there is a polar star by which in this world it guides its frail bark over the ocean of life. As the speed of a body may be so great that the distance over which it passes is imperceptible, so it is with the mind. In the twinkling of an eye it travels to whatever part of creation it pleases—and the eye of the mind possesses magnifying powers that no distance can elude.

I have no doubt but that at this very moment Dr. Dick and Dr. Nichol are travelling from star to star with their telescopes. I have learned from these star-gazers much useful reflection. These rolling wheels, which are a feeble representation of the revolving spheres, say I shall yet see them in the old world. Like a child I would sit at their feet and learn wisdom. A few hours ago I felt nothing but the monotony of the scene—now, new beauties are seen in every spray and new glories in the sky. This is the very place where one can realize something on which the soul can live. Say what you will, I feel like a man. The ocean has turned slave, and bears us on its back to a distant land. The mightiest element is conquered by man, and its waves in humiliating agony die groaning at his feet. I feel a more vital current running through my veins when I reflect that some part of me is immortal. What if fleets and navies are sometimes engulphed in the sea, and thousands go down to people its caverns,—the mind, the soul, yet lives, and must live on though the last billow should howl its wail of woe for the expiring stars. Every strip of sail, every rope, every spar, and every revolution of the paddle, echoes the sentiment that man is immortal. Every breath of steam and every clash of polished steel in this wonderful machine that is urging us onward, tells me that man alone is next to God. The forests may wave their heads, and the mighty rivers may roll on, singing their songs of exultation—yet are they but the emblem of human majesty and greatness. The mountains may rise to the sky, or pierce the home of the Great Spirit—yet man is the one for whom this world is made, and who was made for a world higher than this. The ocean may be his burial-place, or the wide earth may become one vast cemetery, where rich and poor, master and slave, civilized and savage, with friends and enemies, lie side by side. No distinction now! Sleep on, ye generations, sleep! Over your graves I shall yet stray. A day in weeping or laughing, and then I too will haste away. O ye bright worlds that are now waiting, embrace the good who are departing! Ye stars, when ye "shout for joy," say to the departing spirit, "Your toils are ended."

I could stay in this place all night, and feast my soul with contemplation. The dew and the spray are dampening the deck, the passengers have all gone to rest, and I too must seek my resting-place.

CHAPTER III.

THE OCEAN.

THE morning dawns—but old Neptune is either asleep or has gone to visit some "watering place" at the north. The red-faced sun rises out of the sea, and I greet him with a fraternal welcome. Majestically he ascends the eastern slope, and claims the whole azure sky as his kingdom. His rays are pencilled on a floating canvass of clouds, which the skilful fancy would fain weave into the most beautiful drapery. If Sol would only paint such a picture of sea and sky on the canvass over my head as I now behold!—But there is a daguerreotype of it on my memory which the sun-light will not fade.

An iceberg ahead! I have read of icebergs, but this is the first I ever saw. It towers high, like the sail of a ship. I cannot look at it without associating it with the ill-fated "President." A thousand distressing images present themselves at the thought that she may have been sunk by such an iceberg. The screams and groans of the dying, mingled with the sudden letting off of steam and the roaring of the waters, as she sank to rise no more—I will not think of it! There was one on board who stirred the souls of men with holy zeal, but whose heart, burning on the altar of his God, was quenched in the merciless waters. That noble soul was George Cookman. Those eyes which electrified assemblies with their glance, are set like stars in the ocean. Those hands which with their gestures threw a magic spell over the spectators, are perished forever. That voice which stirred the fourtain of feeling to its very depths, is hushed, and the sea-shell whispers his dirge on the deep. But his memory still lives in our hearts. His stirring eloquence breathes the same spirit as of yore. The vestments of his high-born thoughts, and the imagery with which he surrounded himself, proclaim his genius. The knowledge diffused in his ardent desire for the good of others, is still spreading. The ideas which he awakened in the minds of others are extending themselves, for as there is no bound set to the progress of truth so there is no limit to the pursuit of it. Eternity must be shortened and infinity must contract its empire, before the rays of truth will cease to fly onward. The influence of this one man will cause heaven to widen its domains; and like a grain falling into the earth the soul will there multiply itself, having laid its body in the dust and ascended to its God.

"The soul on earth is an immortal guest,
Compelled to starve at an unreal feast;
A spark which upward tends by nature's force;
A stream, divided from its parent source;
A drop, dissevered from the boundless sea;
A moment, parted from eternity;
A pilgrim, panting for the rest to come;
An exile, anxious for his native home."

It is calculated that at the close of this day we shall be near the middle of the Atlantic, between the Old World and the New, and then I am to read a letter which was not to be opened until the first half of the voyage had been accomplished. On its back was written—

"To Kahgegagahbowlk,

Present.

N. B. Not to be opened and read until half-way over, on his voyage to Europe.

By his friend J. S. A."

I have had my curiosity excited to know what was in it, for an Indian has *some* curiosity, though he does not show it by opening his eyes and mouth unmercifully, as refined and polite nations do, who have more manners than the red man.

Soon after sunset I was informed that we were half-way over the sea, which is not what the sailor always means by "half-seas-over." I walked to the bow of the boat, and there stood, looking about me on all sides. Before me, nothing could I see—behind me I could see nothing but the faint track of the steamer—on my right, nothing was to be seen, and on my left, there was no visible object. Above me the stars shone brightly, and beneath me was the dark blue sea. Here is mid ocean; I can imagine myself suspended between the Old World and the New, at the distance of 1500 miles in each direction. The ocean where we are now—O how deep it is! How is my soul oppressed with the feeling of immensity! A sea without visible limits—this is something which without knowledge cannot be contemplated without terror. Here is a place to think of the Great Spirit, and to feel him near you. For the first time, I felt awed by the thought that though man may subdue the sea, yet God is greater than man. Like the petrel over the stormy sea, man roams the ocean of life, tossed and agitated by a thousand anxieties.

This is about half-way. The waves are rocking our faithful boat as if they thought it might now take a little rest. The sea sings a lullaby like the tree-tops in my native forests. I dream of land again, where summer never forsakes the plains, and where spring never forsakes the beautiful vales. Rivers swell their tides eternally, and mountains clothed in nature's own garb, lose their tops in the clouds—this is the land for the Indian.

"Alas that dreams are only dreams!
That fancy cannot give
A lasting beauty to those forms
Which scarce a moment live."

2*

CHAPTER IV.

IRISH CHANNEL AND COAST.

Awoke and got up at 4 o'clock, having slept but little. The light-house appeared abreast of us, and the Cape on our right. What a relief it is to see land again! The shore is barren, and the country perfectly naked. The Island on our left has a house on it, and a small patch of cultivated land.

The sky is hazy, and the atmosphere has a foggy appearance. The hills on the Irish coast are desolate-looking objects. Cold Ireland!—yet a land of warm hearts! A country of famine, yet full of that natural witticism which makes one "laugh and grow fat." The hills appear bold, and so naked that I shudder at the idea of living in such a country.

I have heard a great deal about Erin. The fortunes of the Irish are as varied as those of my own people—the history of both is mostly a history of misfortunes. The Irishman has nobly struggled against the tide of adversity that has been bearing him downward, and though physically defeated, he is in mind unconquered, and has still a *name* in the world.

On our right are the hills of "ould Ireland," and we are nearing the famous Giant's Causeway. The cultivated parts of the shore appear in dots, and we are near enough to see the "huts," about which so much has been said in ridicule and commiseration. Pointing with our spy-glass in the direction of the houses, we see men and women, and children running about the huts. Spot after spot is green, and the crops of the year are beginning to be gathered. The fields of "Murphys," the staple food of the Irish, can be seen.

What a delightful morning greets us on our entering the *Irish Channel!* This channel I have read and heard about, and now, in the many associations with which it is connected in my voyage to the Old World, it will never be forgotten. The channel is covered with sails, and sprinkled here and there with ducks. The sky is now clear as far as a sky in this country *can* be, for I have heard much of the fogginess of Ireland.

Looking over the hills, I say to myself, "This is Paddy land!" and the very thought of Paddy is so full of drollery that I laugh outright when I think of the genuine wit of the Irish. I have had in my native land, reasons to thank the Irish, for when I have met an Irish gentleman I have found a gentleman indeed—high-minded, generous, and noble!

This is the Emerald Isle which I have seen the emigrant in Canada weep for! A love of country is in my breast! There is none so devoid of feeling but that at times he sighs for home; and in my own country I have seen this people weep, wringing their hands, while they talked of Cork, the scenery of Killarney, the famed Blarney-stone, and a thousand other things. This people have two peculiarities, *wit* and *feeling*, which together make *eloquence*, for which they are so celebrated. The heart's blood of the Irishman is warm: his passions sometimes overrule his better judgment. There is a noble daring in his nature which is not easily extinguished. The sweet flower of hospitality is forever budding in his dwelling, however low and humble it may be. There is a queer drollery in each corner of his mouth and eyes. His life is full of great vicissitudes.

This is the land which gave birth to O'Connell, the fiery fagot of eloquence! His tongue fanned the fire of Patriotism, and bathed a nation in tears. O'Connell stood pre-eminent in the British Parliament until his death. When he spoke, the shaggy mane of the British Lion gave evidence of the magnetism of his oratory. The tears of O'Connell mingled with the tears of the two Houses, and of the Reporters, who could not help weeping at the recital of Ireland's misfortunes. The warm hearts of his people justly loved him. This carries me back to a scene which I witnessed in Canada, and which, though common, made a strong impression upon me.

On the afternoon of a certain day, quite late in the Fall, my father and I, being on a hunting excursion, paused before the cabin of a settler, and soon we heard the peculiar brogue of the Irish inviting us to come in. My father lighted his pipe and was going out, when the man of the cabin insisted he should sit down. The scanty appearance of straw in one corner told the amount they had of this world's goods. "Sit down, master, sit down wid me." My father took a seat, and then commenced a queer conversation. From all that I could learn from my imperfect knowledge of English, he was trying to impress my father with the greatness of Daniel O'Connell, his achievements in Ireland, and his speeches in the British Parliament. My father understood only a few words of English: "no" and "yes" were the only ones he used in his responses. The Irishman would show how O'Connell stood while addressing the British Lords, and then with a significant look say to my father, "You think O'Connell a great man?" My father with a shake of the head answered "no," not knowing which of the two words in his vocabulary ought to be used. "You say *no?*" "Yes," said my father, with a nod, very innocently confessing to having used that word instead of "yes." But the enraged Irishman thought all the while that my father depreciated the Statesman of his native land. "You mean 'yes,' eh?" "Yes," said my father with a smile that seemed to deprecate the Irishman's vengeance; and this ended the interview, which was as warm as the heart of an Irishman would admit of without coming to blows.

This incident of my boyhood rushes into my head as fresh as if it had happened just now; but at that time little did I expect ever to see the land of this race of people. Now here it is! its cold bleak hills towering above the mist which creeps along the edge of the shore, and winding ravines full of huts clustering together.

Having rested but little last night, I fell asleep, and to my utter disappointment when I awoke we had passed the Giant's Causeway! and I could only have a glimpse of it as it receded in the distance.

Ships are seen all over the surface of the channel. It is very still and calm. How aggravating it must be to see us shoot by them and they almost stationary! Various cities of Ireland appear on our right. The sky is full of fog,—and on our left we see Scotland. Numerous sea-birds are flying around us.

I am determined to see the Blarney-stone some day. Weary and tired though I am, and with aching eyes, I must sit down to write a note to my father.

"No-say.

"Me quach ne de nain ne mah owh Monedo. Tah que she non Omah. Me nwah bah me nah quod sah Ewh Odah keem Ewh Me ne seno we ne neh." (I had better not write this letter in Indian, on the pages of this book, for fear some one will come on me for damages for the breaking of his jaw while trying to speak the words.)

THE INTERPRETATION.

"Father.

"I thank the Great Spirit that I have arrived here safe. I am now in the land of the Irishman. By its looks I should think it a very pleasant land."

At 2 o'clock we see the Isle of Man. On our left, steamboat sails in view at a distance.

5 o'clock. The steamer for America is now in sight Our signal hoisted, "The President is dead!" and the captain of the steamer read the signal. "Sir Robert Peel is dead," was the answer.

At 10 o'clock we see the lights along the docks, and our guns repeat the sound with which we parted from the wharf of Boston, 'bang,' 'bang,' 'bang,' with two others added, by which the people will expect to hear something more than usual by this steamer. The line of lights makes a splendid appearance, and if the docks are equal in extent what must I think of the commerce of this city? We dropped anchor a short time before 12 o'clock.

This is Liverpool.

We meet some of those who preceded us to this country.

Sunday morning. I hunted among those to whom I carried letters for some one who would invite me to attend church with him, and was fortunate enough to succeed. Spoke in the afternoon. Encountered a few dozen beggars in the street on my way to church. I find it hard to get small change for them all.

CHAPTER V.

ARRIVAL—STRANGE THINGS AND PEOPLE—DOCKS—SHIPS, ETC.

THE Liverpool Times announced my arrival in the following language:

"A CHIEF OF THE OJIBWAY NATION.—The steam-ship Niagara, which arrived on Saturday last, brought over to this country the Rev. George Copway, or Kah-Ge-Ga-Gah-Bowh, a chief of the Ojibway nation. Twelve years ago he was a hunter in the woods of America, but having obtained his education at the expense of some benevolent gentleman of the state of Illinois, during the years 1838–9, he returned to his nation, determined to labor for the elevation of his tribe. He has devised a scheme for concentrating and civilizing the American Indians of the north-west, upon territory to be purchased by the free contributions of the American people; and we understand he intends shortly to hold a meeting in this town with the view of explaining the object at which he aims. He is a fine, noble-looking man, very intelligent, and speaks the English language with great fluency, correctness, and elegance. He purposes attending the Peace Congress at Frankfort, and his stay here will necessarily be very limited. He sat on the bench with Mr. Rushton, on Wednesday last, for a short time, and appeared to take great interest in the proceedings of the Police Court."

To Mr. Baines the Editor of the Times, and to the Editors of the other papers, I am indebted for the kind manner in which they came forward to place me before the citizens of Liverpool and the British public in general.

This, then, is a part of England. How crowded are the streets! What large truck horses! with plenty of omnibuses and noisy beggars; and worse than all, the shaving hack-drivers. Beardless as I am comparatively, they yet manage to shave me.

Sabbath morning, I went to see the Rev. Mr. Pennell, brother of a friend of mine in New York. This gentleman's kindness was serviceable to me in a great many ways—I shall not forget it. We attended a meeting out of town in the rural district of Seacombe. The Old World being new to me, my first business will be to make observation of things, and to describe them as I see them. Like a new being on the stage of life, I must gather the materials for future reflection. I am now a school-boy, and I shall study the English character, and learn if possible some of its many noble qualities.

Now, after five days, gazing, I have seen something of the English. How kind they are! The name of Charles Sumner, of Boston, is here justly appreciated, for wherever I have delivered the letters from this gentleman I have met with a cordial reception.

I am snugly housed with the Rev. G. Pennell. The Mersey river sweeps before me, ebbing and flowing with the sea. The view of the harbor is beautiful! Before these several items of interest grow cold I will sit down and write a friend in Boston, the Rev. Mr. Norris, for I must still send "paper talk" to my American friends, though I am 3,000 miles from them.

LIVERPOOL, July 27th, 1850.

My Dear Friend :—I am now in a strange place. The country, the people, and the places are strange. The sky is strange—indeed the waters before my window roll with strange rapidity. The steamboats look strange, black, miserable things—the wretched ferry-boats are the worst things of all.

The recollection of the ocean is grateful to me, for never did I dream that I should ever have such a pleasant journey over the "big waters" as I did. Fair winds, clear skies, and no rolling sea—calm as the waters of our *dear* "Hudson," that beloved river, which winds along (as Byron said of such scenery,)

"In the wild power of mountain majesty."

The Port of Liverpool. From my window I can see a thousand ships. They appear like forest trees, their masts towering between me and the great city. The tide, rising higher here than in America, rolls in and out rapidly before me, and the diversity of ships sweep in a mighty phalanx, on each side of the river. I can see all kinds of boats, from a yawl to a steamship. The steamboats run here on these waters nearly as often as our omnibuses in the streets of Boston. But how wretched they are! no cover overhead at all. The rain comes down without mercy, and the rain here is dirty and smoky enough.

The port is admirably well calculated to accommodate several thousand ships more. The flags of all nations appear here, and none wave more proudly than "the stars and stripes." These flash from sea to sea, and roll on, over every wave. One half the commerce is under the flag of America.

We brought the news of the death of the President of the United States, into this country. The next day all the American ships had their flags half-mast, and the papers from all the principal towns of the kingdom are filled with regrets at his departure. He seems to have been esteemed very highly in this country—all creeds speak well of him. Great anxiety is felt as to what course Mr. Fillmore will take with reference to the exciting questions of the day.

The Docks of Liverpool. Of the celebrity of these you have already heard. They are a piece of master workmanship—a noble monument of untiring industry. The tide brings in a hundred ships inside, and when it goes out, it takes with it as many more. There, within the reach of the streets which run from the town into the river, are hid secure the ships which have braved the oceans of all quarters of the world. Here, now, as if weary of wandering by sea, slumber the god-like instruments of navigation. I can hear the peculiar cry of the sailor, now while I write.

I felt *so small* when the captain told us that we were about half-way over the sea. What! nothing around us but the blue, clear sky, and the mighty caverns beneath us! To be suspended thus, is not so pleasant. But, how secure did I feel there, when I knew that God was near! His arms were around us. We shall praise him.

The town of Liverpool is a rusty-looking place at first; but the better acquainted you are with the place, the better you like it. The streets are mostly narrow, compared with ours in America. Liverpool appears to be almost as large as New York.

The town police is a well-regulated arrangement. The policemen march to duty just as the soldiers do. They wear black clothes, high hats and glazed at the rim. There must be several thousands of them, for they appear to be in every place. The smoke of the town, or in fact of the whole country, is like the smoke of Pittsburg.

I have just commenced with the *H*inglish, in receiving their hospitality, having already been in the country, to the mansions of these Liverpool merchants. I find everything in a tasteful order—the parks, gardens, hedges, ponds filled with fish, &c., are all in array, as it were, to entice the very angels from the skies.

My cause is here warmly advocated by the papers, and I hope to realize the whole of what I had anticipated from these noble English people. I meet with nothing but kindness. I expect to deliver an address before the Mayor and merchants, at 11 o'clock, A. M., on Monday, and lay my plan before the people, at the Merchants' Exchange Rooms.

The Peace Congress does not meet until the 22d of August, and I shall visit Manchester and London before then. Afterwards I go to Glasgow and Edinburgh, and devote two weeks to France. It is my present purpose to return in November.

I have only written about the port, docks, town, &c., without much about the people. I must reserve that for another time.

My dear friend, do *enjoy* America while I am away for *me too*, will you? and I will see all *the sights* in Europe for you, in exchange. Farewell! Yours faithfully,

[G. COPWAY, Ojibway Nation.

The common things which interest and arrest one's attention are numerous—the town enveloped in smoke; the docks stretching away for over six miles; the ferry-boats, smoky, black and dirty—no covers to them. The rain is suffered to come down without any conscience on the heads of old and young, and the soot falls on your linen, or on your face, until you make beautiful, fine, delicate streaks across your cheeks and nose in wiping the sweat from your forehead.

I see much form and order in everything which concerns the conduct of the people. Every lamp-post must have a guard, as if it were an object of great interest and importance, and every corner is more or less favored with the presence of a policeman.

None of the well-informed have the impudence which shows itself in asking endless questions. All the impudence of the country seems concentrated in the street-beggar, who is the very personification of this questionable virtue. These scape-goats from Purgatory have for nearly a week watched the door of the Waterloo Hotel. They know where green ones resort, and there they gather together like silk-worms on a mulberry. How gracefully they doff their hats! with what mock reverence they uncover their heads! They bend the knee for a "Penny, please, sir!" Having received one, another comrade is sent on the same errand, until you have given pennies to a company of a dozen beggars, and this only sharpens their appetite. To get rid of this humanity in rags I gave away many a penny when I landed, but this only brought more.

The Waterloo House, the Adelphi, and other large Hotels, are guarded for the special accommodation of the rich by enormous charges. Although I have nothing to say in favor of this, I can assure any of our Americans travelling this way, that they will find all things right at the Waterloo, and the keeper, Mr. Lynn, a fine-hearted gentleman.

My experience has taught me that Hotel servants in this country are constant plagues. I am resolved not to be annoyed by them. If any charges for servants are to be made I mean to have it *included* in the Bill—for when you call for your bill the charge is made out for lodging and meals only. Then come the servants like a regiment of starved turkeys clamoring for food. First the Porter, with an air of dignity,

"Please remember the *Porter*, sir."

How much?

"2*s*. 6*d*. sir."—(about 62½ cts.) *Paid.*

"Please remember the *Chamber-maid*, sir," says another.

How much?

"I get 2*s*. 6*d*. sir."—*Paid.*

"Please remember the *Bootblack*, sir."

How much?

"2*s*. sir."—*Paid.*

"Please remember the *Errand-boy*," says a boy, touching his cap.

How much?

"2*s*. sir."—*Paid.*

Here comes a man with a whip in his hand, and touches his cap to his forehead.

"Please pay for *l——lo——looking at my carriage!*" Job is said to have had a greal deal of patience, but sure I am he never was in England.

Were I allowed to give advice to these Hotel keepers, I would say, "When you make out your bills, put in your charge for Servants' hire and all, and do not trouble us Americans with such intrusions, for our time is precious."

CHAPTER VI.

THE PEOPLE—TOWN—COUNTRY.

On Sabbath last, in the morning, I first saw Liverpool. I have since visited the docks, public buildings and institutions. One week has nearly elapsed, and I am announced to speak twice on Sunday, the 29th, which is to-morrow.

Mr. Richard Rathbone and his brother, the ex-mayor of Liverpool, have been unremitting in their kind attentions to me. I shall never forget the beautiful country residences of these gentlemen. The wild woods of "Woodcote" shall ever have a place in my memory. There I have just been entertained in company with the chief magistrate of Liverpool, E. Rushton, and four or five counsellors-at-law. The lovely pond girded with grass and shrubbery, the beautifully shaded walks, the exquisite flowers—how shall I begin to describe them?

My friend Richard Rathbone's house is in the centre of this lovely little kingdom. On Thursday evening I stood amid the foliage of the trees and saw the sun sinking in the midst of gorgeous clouds, its golden rays reflected on the sky and the scenery around me, and then I realized the appropriateness of a description that had before been only a picture in my imagination.

> "How soft the green bank sloping down from the hill
> To the spot where the fountain grew suddenly still!
> How cool was the shadow the long branches gave
> As they hung from the willow, and dipped in the wave!
> And then each pale lily, that slept in the stream
> Rose and fell with a wave, as if stirred by a dream."

I left a delightful reality for a remembrance when the carriage drove me away from this place. May the sunshine of heaven ever rest upon it.

Next day, I must go and visit the family of William Rathbone, the ex-mayor. In the lovely spot where I shall see them, the flowers and shrubbery of all lands are growing. "Green Bank"—how appropriate the appellation! Here we must feast again, I suppose: the very thoughts of such a groaning board makes me groan inwardly, and the recollection of such fearful inroads upon the dainties of the table gives me a leaning in that direction.

A Reverend gentleman dined with us, and my fondest anticipations as to the dinner were fully realized. After enjoying a walk about the grounds I had reluctantly to leave, for other engagements. Mr. Rathbone is truly one of nature's noblemen.

The Liverpool Standard, on Thursday morning, announced our presence and arrival, as follows:—

"AN INDIAN CHIEF.—By the Niagara steam-ship, an Indian chief of the Ojibway nation, named Kah-ge-ga-gah-bowkh, arrived in this town. He is on his way to the Peace Congress, at Frankfort, and will only make a short stay in Liverpool. His adopted name is George Copway. We were yesterday introduced to him, and found him a very intelligent man. His complexion is of course rather dark, and his hair long and black, and he is a tall, well-proportioned, and handsome man, with the manners and graceful dignity of a perfect gentleman. We hail his presence amongst us as a token of spreading intelligence among the North American Indians. We give in another column a well-written poem composed for Mr. Copway and recited by him on board the Niagara.

GEORGE COPWAY

(KAH-GE-GA-GAH-BOWH.)

We may also mention that we had placed in our hands two volumes from the pen of our North American friend, one of his own life, entitled, 'History of a Child of the Forest, and of his Nation,' and the other a poetic sketch of 'the bravery and prowess of the Ojibway nation.' Both works proclaim their author to be a man of close observation, of original thought, and of sound judgment."

I have learned that the Peace Congress does not sit until the 22d, 23d, and 24th, of next month ; and now I shall have a little time to visit the different towns. I will have one invariable set of rules to observe wherever I shall be during my stay in this country—and it is this.

I will uphold my race—I will endeavor never to say nor do anything which will prejudice the mind of the British public against my people—In this land of refinement I will be an Indian—I will treat everybody in a manner that becomes a gentleman—I will patiently answer all questions that may be asked me—I will study to please the people, and lay my own feelings to one side.

Since I have to be in the country so long before going to the Peace Congress, I will deliver some lectures and addresses before the people, and endeavor if possible to interest them in reference to the present condition and prospects of the Indian races in America, and to give them some idea of what we have been doing for the civilization of the Red man.

Sabbath day. I had to speak for the Rev. Mr. Hall, in Birkenhead—A very pleasant time—the people are easily affected—they appear to enjoy themselves. I spoke to another audience this afternoon; and I must soon speak to another. I see people flocking to the house . . . . Yes —it was crowded. A very good building, and seats circular—I hope some good is done.

One thing I have noticed with regret in this country; and that is, the agitation of the Wesleyans. There seems to be a division on the subject of government and discipline of this body. Many have asked me which side of the agitation I belong to. My answer has been, *I know no side.* The church government of the Methodists in England and America has been rather too coercive. Too much power is lodged in the hands of the Ministers, and here it has resulted in a rupture all over the country. The papers are full of it; and the organs of the two sections show that there is a great deal of bitterness of feeling on both sides. They run one another down, while each one praises itself. The struggle has commenced, and no one can tell when nor where the controversy will end. The ministers have no desire of losing their power by acceding to the wishes of the minority. The others are persevering in their demands for a reformation, somewhere, for the good of the whole—and English-like, one is just as obstinate as the other.

One thing which seems to be a source of misunderstanding with them, is this—the trying of members by the Rules for the temporal regulation of the Church, and condemning them by these rules, and thus reading them out of the churches, which is said to be making the rules for the better temporal government of a church, *paramount to the laws of God.* Whether this is the case I cannot say, but it is the impression I receive from all that I have heard said on the subject.

I was to have given a lecture at the Commercial Sales' Room, but it was attended by gentlemen and no ladies, or at most only two or three. The lecture was then postponed, and the meeting was appointed at the Mechanics' Institute, where I am to deliver my next lecture.

Though I am constantly busy, time slips by me so rapidly that I can accomplish but little—and now for the meeting. The house was crammed, and the people well packed—a good room for speaking in it is too. On Thursday morning, among the papers that noticed my lecture was the Mercury. I shall give the entire report.

NORTH AMERICAN INDIANS.

Last evening a meeting was held in the Mechanics' Institution, to hear the Rev. George Copway, a chief of the Ojibway Indians, explain his scheme for concentrating the Indians of North America on the northwest frontier of the United States. There was a very large attendance.

Mr. WM. RATHBONE occupied the chair, and after a few preliminary remarks, introduced Mr. Copway to the meeting.

The Rev. Mr. COPWAY then came forward, and was enthusiastically received by the meeting. After some introductory remarks, he proceeded to state what were the causes which caused the Indians to decrease, and why they had not improved. There had been an idea amongst the pale faces that the Indians were a doomed race: there seemed to be something over their heads, and therefore they would not lift their hands to extricate the Indians. One of the reasons which caused a decrease in the number of Indians was the diseases which had been introduced into their country by Europeans, such as small-pox, and other diseases, which their simple medicines and limited knowledge were unable to cure; and not only had their number been diminished by disease, but also by wars amongst themselves, and since European arms had been introduced amongst them the mortality in their affrays had been greatly augmented. The wars which had taken place between the European nations in America had also thinned the number of Indians. The fourth cause of their diminution was the use of ardent spirits, one of the greatest curses which had been introduced into their country by the white man.—(Applause.) He instanced two or three cases in which the most destructive results had been caused to the Indians by the free use of ardent spirits, and yet the white man philosophically said this was all Providence. He sometimes trembled for the people of the United States, though he hoped never to have the same feeling as when he was on the war trail. The Indians occupied no half-way ground. When they professed to be Christians they would be found to be so.—(Applause.) He now came to the reasons why the Indians had not improved. The reasons why they had not improved were that no sooner had they a school established, and they began to cultivate the ground, than they were forced to give up their land and go further west; and sometimes when they refused to give up their land the most nefarious means were resorted to to compel them to do so. The first great reason, therefore, why they had not improved was that they were not allowed to remain on their land long enough. The next reason why the Indian did not improve, was that the education offered to him was not suitable to his habits. They should adapt their institutions in accordance to the feelings of the Indians. The Indian did not wish to be driven into anything by the rod: his common sense would lead him, without being driven, or being made the machine; and this was one reason why the Indian had not fallen in love with education. The next reason why the Indian did not improve was, that the manner of introducing education to him was very peculiar. The Missionary endeavored to translate English works into the Indian language, instead of teaching the Indian youth the English language, and thus introduce them to the broad sea of intelligence. He had been overruled on this subject ten years ago; but they were then beginning to see the value of his suggestion. The next reason why the Indian did not improve was, that the Missionaries did not take the wisest course for introducing Christianity. When they sent Missionaries amongst the Indians, they should teach them to love one another before they went amongst them. If they did this they would save a great deal of trouble; but he implored of them to send none but men who followed the precepts of the Saviour, not only by preaching, but by practising them from their hearts.—(Applause.) Above all, Missionaries should be impressed with the glorious and noble principles of Christianity, and do not send narrow-hearted bigots.—(Applause.) He then proceeded to state his plan for the concentration of the Indians, which was that the Indians of the northwest, consisting of about one hundred thousand souls, should be granted forever about 150 square miles of territory, between the falls of St. Anthony and the West of Winosotah, and by giving the Indians a permanent settlement in this land, induce them to become farmers, and learn the arts of peace and civilization. If this was not done in the course of forty years there would not be a buffalo left on this side of the Rocky Mountains; and then, he asked, on what would the Indians live? If they touched a herd of cattle belonging to the American settlers, the war-whoop would be raised against the Indians, and they would be exterminated. It was to prevent this that he had brought forward this scheme. The Indian would then have a home, where he could till his land and impart instruction to his offspring; fearing no removal. When he had the fee simple of this land he would feel himself treated as a man, and he would act as a man.—(Applause.) The Indian would then be no longer a trouble. It might have been thought presumptuous in him to start such a scheme, but when he saw his brethren being destroyed by inches, he could not hesitate to offer himself as a sacrifice for his brethren; and he had come to England, not to get an expression of feeling all over the country, or for the purpose of raising their noble patriotism to urge on the Government of America; he would rather not receive a gift from any one having a feeling of this sort.—(Hear.) He wanted the people to know the real position of the Indian, and he wanted the parents of every child of the Great Spirit to whisper to them to pray for the poor Indian, that God might shower his mercies on him, and that, when the poor Indian warrior died, he might see his children mounting their way up the high hill of noble greatness, and that when he died he might wake in a world of endless bliss in the skies. In prosecuting this matter it required means, and it was mainly for this purpose that he wished to get the people interested ; and if he could get, say £2,500, which he expected to do during the coming Congress, in the month of December, he would return to Washington again, and he intended to send out three of his brethren to deliver addresses throughout the country, and at the same time to have blank petitions circulated, and at a certain given time, in the month of January or February, he wanted to touch the wires which vibrated from one end of the country to the other, he wanted to besiege the white house of the Government of the United States, and knock at the door of the American Government, that justice might be done to the Indian by giving him a home from which he shall never be removed again.—(Applause.) After referring to the kindness which he had experienced at the hands of Mr. Richard Rathbone, and expressing the pleasure which he felt at seeing so large a meeting before him, the reverend gentleman gave a very graphic and poetical description of an aged Indian, who, harassed with care, addressed his children to the following effect : —There is no rest in this country ; the white man is come, and he is powerful. There is only one place beyond the setting sun. You will soon see me die. The lecturer then repeated the following lines :—

I will go to my tent and lie down in despair;
I will paint me with black, and will sever my hair;
I will go to the shore where the hurricane blows,
And reveal to the God of the tempest my woes ;
I will for a season on bitterness feed,
For my kindred are gone to the mounds of the dead:
They died not by hunger, nor wasting decay,
The steel of the white man hath swept them away.

Mr. Copway concluded by expressing his gratitude for the kindness manifested by the Liverpool public, adding that whatever donations any persons might think proper to present, in support of the cause, they would be thankfully received. A friend, in this town, told Mr. Copway that he would give £25 towards the object, and wished it every prosperity. The reverend lecturer was listened to with breathless attention, and resumed his seat amid the most deafening applause.

The Chairman said, that after the very excellent address they had heard, there must be shown something more substantial than clapping and cheering. He also stated that it should be understood that with the general treatment of the Americans towards the Indians they had nothing to do. After a powerful appeal, from the chairman, urging individuals to come forward and contribute their mite towards so philanthropic an object, many persons responded to the call, and their names were entered on the subscription list.

CHAPTER VII.

HISTORICAL NOTICES OF LIVERPOOL.

[These notices are gathered from a small volume—Black's Railway Map.]

LIVERPOOL, the second city in the kingdom of Great Britain, is situated on the right side of the Mersey. A castle is said to have been built here by Roger of Poictiers, which was demolished in 1659. St. Georges' Church now stands on the site. During the civil wars, Liverpool held out against Prince Rupert for a month, but at last it was taken, and many of the garrison and the inhabitants were put to the sword. The town was very soon after retaken by Colonel Birch, and continued to remain true to the popular cause.

Liverpool was merely a chapelry attached to the parish of Walton, till the reign of William III., and in 1650 there were only fifteen ships belonging to the port.

It was deeply engaged in the African slave-trade; and in 1764, more than half this trade was carried on by the merchants of Liverpool.

Since the great extension of the Cotton Manufacture, it has become the port where the great bulk of the raw material is received, and whence the exports of manufactured goods are chiefly made to all parts of the world. It also enjoys a very large proportion of the trade between England and Ireland, especially since the employment of steam-vessels for the conveyance of merchandise.

Liverpool is supposed to possess one-twelfth part of the shipping of Great Britain; one-fourth part of the foreign trade; one-sixth part of the general commerce; and one half as much trade as the port of London. The custom dues are between four and five millions sterling; the Cotton imported reaching a million and a half of bags. The imports are about twenty milions in value, the exports exceeding that sum by a fourth, and it is calculated that 1600 tons of goods pass daily between Liverpool and Manchester. About two fifths of the tonnage inwards and outwards are engaged in the trade with the United States. Considerable traffic is also carried on with the West India Islands, Brazil, and other parts of South

America, and the East Indies. Its intercourse with Ireland is about equal in amount with that kept up with every port in Great Britain. The inland trade of Liverpool is much assisted by means of canals and railways, and it has benefited more than any port in Great Britain (London excepted) from the application of steam power to navigation. The docks are constructed on the most stupendous scale. They consist of wet, dry, and graving docks, and are connected with wide and commodious quays, and immense warehouses. The wet docks occupy a water superficies of 90 acres, 3384 yards, and the quays measure 7 miles 156 yards in length.

Until about fifty years ago, the streets of Liverpool were narrow and inconvenient, and the buildings devoid of architectural beauty, but successive improvements have given to the town an elegance not to be met with in any other commercial port in the kingdom. The most important public buildings are, the town hall, the exchange building, and the custom house. The town hall is a handsome Palladian building, surmounted by a dome, which is crowned by a statue of Britannia. It contains a number of portraits, and a statue of Roscoe, by Chantry, and on the landing of the staircase there is a statue of

Canning, by the same artist. The interior of the town hall, besides the rooms on the basement story, contains a saloon, two drawing rooms, two ball rooms, a banqueting room, and a refectory, the whole elegantly fitted up.

The Exchange buildings form three sides of a square, in the centre of which is a group of statuary, in memory of Nelson, executed by Westmacott in 1813. The new custom house, by far the finest building in Liverpool, both in magnitude and architectural execution, contains also the post office, the excise office, the stamp office, the dock treasurer's and secretary's offices, the board room and offices of the dock committee.

At the junction of London Road and Pembroke Place, there is an equestrian statue of George III., by Westmacott.

St. James' Cemetery was once a quay of red stone, and consists principally of catacombs. On the summit of the rock, near the entrance, is a beautiful chapel, containing some good sculpture. Here the late Mr. Huskisson was interred, and a monument to his memory has been placed over the spot, with a statue of fine white marble, habited in a toga.

Liverpool contains thirty-two places of worship connected with the Establishment, and fifty-nine belonging to the Dissenters of various denominations. There are in Liverpool, 75 Sunday Schools, with 16,000 scholars; 43 evening Schools, with 548 scholars; 648 day Schools, with 28,916 scholars; there are 13 Medical charities, 12 provident, and 23 religious. There are 15 literary institutions, 12 places of public amusement, and 10 prisons. Among the literary institutions may be mentioned the Royal Institution, formed in 1814 by Mr. Roscoe—the Literary and Scientific, and Commercial Institution set on foot in 1835—the Mechanic's Institution, opened in 1837—the Liverpool Institution of Fine Arts—the Atheneum—the Lyceum—the Collegiate Institution, &c.

The markets of Liverpool are very remarkable structures; that of St. John occupies nearly two acres of ground, the whole under one roof, supported by 116 pillars.

The Zoological Gardens comprise ten acres of ground, and are laid out with a great degree of taste.

The manufactures of Liverpool are not important. There are several sugar refineries, some small foundries, a good deal of ship building in wood and iron, a manufactory of steam engines, anchors, chain cables, and similar articles naturally demanded in a large port.

The value of the corporation estates is estimated at three millions of money, and the annual income derived from rent and dock dues has increased to upwards of £320,000. A great proportion of this income has been devoted to the improvement of the town, including the building of churches and other public edifices. The sum expended in these objects and in widening the streets between 1786 and 1838 amounts to £668,300.

The site of Liverpool is low and unhealthy. According to the Registrar-General's returns of births and deaths, the deaths and marriages are double, while the births are little more than half the numbers of the averages of all England.

In 1700 the population of Liverpool was 4240. In 1841 it was 223,003. It returns two members to Parliament.

The country around Liverpool abounds in every direction with fine residences. Of these the most important are, Knowsley Hall (Earl of Derby); Croxteth Park (Earl of Sefton); Ince Blandell, the seat of the Blandell family; Childwall Abbey (Marquis of Salisbury); Speke

Hall (Mr. Watt); Hall Hall (Mr. Blackbune); Woolton Hall, &c.

At Everton is the cottage where Prince Rupert established his head-quarters when he besieged the town in 1644.

On the morning of July 31st, Mr. Pennell took me to the Mayor, and Sir Elkanor Ermatage.

Manchester, as its name shows (Man-castra) was a Roman station, and is supposed to have taken its rise in the reign of Titus. Under the Saxons it became the abode of a Thane. After the Norman Conquest, William gave the place to William of Poictou. The barony descended to the Grelleys, and the De la Warres, and at length the Manorial rights became vested in the family of Mosley. In the civil wars, Manchester ranged itself on the side of Parliament, and sustained a siege conducted by Lord Strange, afterwards Earl of Derby.

Manchester was distinguished for its manufactures so early as the times of Edward VIII. and Edward VI. At first the woollen was the only branch of trade; but since the middle of the last century, the cotton business has taken the lead, and Manchester has now become the centre of that manufacture. Of late the spinning and weaving of silk have been introduced, and the printing and dyeing of silk are also extensively carried on in this town.

The manufacture of machinery has risen to great importance and perfection in Manchester, and it has also manufactures of linen, small-wares, hats, umbrellas, &c. Its commerce is greatly aided by its communications with almost every part of England, by means of railways and canals. The district in which the town stands contains some of the best coal strata in England; a circumstance to which the place is indebted in no small degree for its prosperity. One of the most interesting buildings in Manchester is the Collegiate Church, a noble Gothic building, containing several chapels and chantries, a richly ornamented choir, a number of monuments, &c. It was built in 1422. The reputed founder was Thomas Lord De la Warre, but several other persons assisted in building it. Considerable additions were made in the sixteenth century, and many alterations and additions are of recent origin.

Of the numerous chapels, all but one are private property. The chapel of the Derby family is that which possesses the greatest share of historic interest.

St. Mary's chapel contains several interesting monuments of the family of the Chathams ; and the Trafford chapel, in addition to the memorials of the ancient family from which it takes its name, possesses a very handsome monument to the memory of Dauntsey Hulme, Esq., a distinguished philanthropist. There are a considerable number of other churches in Manchester, and the church-building society has been formed to promote additional church accommodations. The Dissenters have also numerous places of worship, and Manchester has been long distinguished as possessing a greater dissenting population than any other town in the kingdom.

The ecclesiastical government of Manchester was formerly vested in the warden and four fellows of the Collegiate Church, subsequently elevated to the rank of a cathedral.

The first bishop was consecrated in 1847. The free grammar school of Manchester was founded in the early part of the fifteenth century by Hugh Oldham, Bishop of Exeter, and is very richly endowed, but is far from effecting the good which its splendid resources might produce.

Chetham's Hospital, or the College, was originally

founded by the De la Warres in the reign of Henry VI. After the dissolution, it became the property of the Derby family, and was purchased from the celebrated Countess of Derby, in compliance with the will of Humphry Chetham, an eminent merchant, for the purpose of forming a blue-coat hospital and library. This institution provides for the education and support of eighty poor children. The library consists of about 25,000 volumes, and there is an annual provision for its augmentation. The inhabitants of the town are allowed free access to it under certain regulations. The educational institutions in Manchester have been defective both in number and quality, but great exertions are now making to extend the benefits of instruction to all classes of the community.

There are two Mechanics' Institutions in the town; several Lyceums; an Institution called the Athenæum, a Literary and Philosophical Society, numerous charitable institutions, &c. The other public buildings worthy of notice are, the Exchange, the Infirmary, the Society of Arts or Royal Institution, the Town-Hall, the two Theatres, the new Museum of Natural History, the New Bailey Prison, Manchester Commercial Rooms, &c., &c.

A Botanic Garden was formed here in 1830. There are five railways diverging from Manchester, which furnish the town with the greatest facilities for extending its trade, viz. Liverpool, Leeds, Bolton and Bury, Birmingham and Sheffield Railways. The immense mills, workshops and foundries well deserve a visit from the tourist. Manchester returns two members of Parliament. Its population is 163,856.

CHAPTER VIII.

COMMENCEMENT OF TRAVEL.

THIS morning I find good Lessons from the following, which will be useful alike to all travellers as it will be to me. And here it is from Mr. Black's Railway Guide.

He says,—

"Pack up your luggage in such order that you can readily carry with you the small matters you may want on your journey, or immediately on your arrival; let the rest be put in such trunks, cases, boxes, or other packages as will either effectually protect it, or show at first sight that it must be handled carefully; remembering that, at railway stations, a great deal of business must be done in a little time, and therefore luggage, which seems able to bear it, sometimes gets rough usage.

Let your name and destination appear legibly on your luggage; and if you wish to be safe against all chances of loss, put your name and address inside also of each package. Picture to yourself your trunk lying on the road, left in the corner of an office, or sent out to a wrong direction, and imagine what you would then wish should be on or in it, that it might be correctly and speedily sent to you. What you would then wish you had done, do before you start. Let the label be of a strong material, and firmly attached to the package.

Be at the station some minutes before the time; if you do not resolve to be so, expect to see the train on its way without you.

Get your ticket (by paying your fare), and be careful to understand exactly how far that ticket frees you. On some railways you keep that ticket to the end of your journey; on others you are called on for it at starting. In either case be ready with it, remembering that, if you cannot produce it, you may be called upon to pay your fare again.

See where your luggage is placed on the carriage, and prefer that it should be on that in which you are to be seated, if practicable; see also that the company's ticket or luggage number be affixed to each package, or you may be called on to pay the carriage of it.

Expect to pay for the carriage of all your luggage above 56 lbs. weight.

Take the best care you can to prevent the necessity of your leaving the carriage before you reach the refreshment station at the end of your journey.

Take your seats as soon as you have made all needful arrangements; you may have with you a carpet-bag, hat-box, or other luggage, if it be not so bulky as to annoy your fellow-passengers.

Do not open the carriage doors yourself; and do not at any station, except those where refreshments are provided, attempt to leave the carriage for any reason whatever, without the knowledge of the conductor, lest you be injured by some accident, or left behind.

Neither smoking nor dogs are allowed in the carriages; the latter are conveyed under proper arrangements, and at a small charge, which may easily be learnt at each station.

Female attendants will be found at each terminus, and at the refreshment station, to wait on ladies and children.

Children under ten years of age are conveyed at half-price; only infants unable to walk are carried without charge.

Invalids and decrepit persons commonly receive very considerate attention from the persons employed at the stations and on the line; but they must calculate on none which would materially interfere with the general working of the establishment, except they have expressly applied for, and been assured of, it beforehand.

Carriages of various kinds, special and public, suitable to the different localities, will be found at both the termini, and at nearly all the stations.

On change of carriage, or leaving the train, be careful to see what becomes of your luggage.

Each person employed on the line has a distinguishing number on the collar of his coat; if you have any complaint to make, write to the Secretary, designating the offender by his number.

Railway servants are enjoined to the observance of civility and attention to all passengers, and they usually fulfil these duties very cheerfully when treated with common propriety. They are forbidden to receive any fee or gratuity."

This I shall endeavor to follow in all my travels.

This morning I start for the metropolis. At 9 o'clock the cars move; everything connected with them goes on like clockwork. The depôt is an iron building, covered with glass. Here are men in uniform, at work; they are those who belong to the railway company. The coaches are built differently from those in America. They are calculated more for comfort, at least in summer; but in winter they must be cold, for there is no place for fire in them.

The tunnel through which we pass is over a mile in length, and some distance under ground. Having traversed this artificial cave, the black iron pony starts on his way to London in good earnest. Here we go! whirling, rolling, rattling, whistling, at the rate of 30 miles an hour. Our conductor in uniform wears a watch, and carries in his hand a whistle. With his time-piece he regulates his speed, and with his whistle calls out "all aboard!"—he speaks not, but blows his shrill whistle. This I think is a very good arrangement, for many a time some one speaks as loud as he, and in that case he could not be heard; but no one can imitate the whistle. This therefore is much more suitable than the sailor phrase, "all aboard," to say nothing of the idea which it gives to travelling in a rail-car instead of a steamboat.

But no one can stop to ruminate when being run away with. Here we go! What a beautiful country! I can at least take a bird's-eye view of it. Groups of trees, and cultivated fields spreading as far as the eye can reach, on both sides. Beautiful green hedges, and fields of grain, some being reaped, and some still standing, waving gracefully as if inviting the reapers to the harvest. There is scarcely a spot of land as far as the eye can reach that is not cultivated. Wherever the Englishman discovers land there he must have a farm. How vastly superior in point of cultivation is this country to America! Were they as much superior in cultivation of mind, we might be ashamed of ourselves! Unfortunately, they who till the soil have generally little time, and still less opportunity, for mental improvement. Without this, all this landscape beauty is but an outside shell, and when our country shall have become as old as England now is, we may excel the English in cultivation and refinement.

I could wear out the points of a hundred steel pens in writing the word "beautiful." The garden-like appearance of the whole country ! The architectural appearance of the residences, from the proud castle to the humble cottage, including country seats, churches, farm-houses, and every variety of shelter ! The speedy and perfect arrangement of the railways, and the facility with which the functions of the post-office department are carried on, are surprising. When I see and think of these things, I am half inclined to regret coming to this country, for fear that on my return home I may not love my native wilds as I did before. But whether this will be the effect upon me I shall be able to judge better hereafter, when I shall have seen other parts of the kingdom.

For two hours we have been flying like a blazing comet. We have passed over a rolling country, and found that there are some marshes, even here. The roads traverse in all directions, and are bordered with lovely cottages, through the casements of which we perceive now and then beautiful faces, looking at us as we pass. The road-sides are planted with shade trees, and our eyes are refreshed with the sight of orchards, giving sweet promise of refreshment to the body when their fruits shall have been gathered in. Much pains seems to be taken in the rearing of ornamental trees, and much care bestowed in setting them out and making them subservient to art.

Look at those deep valleys ! and the hills, how lofty and finely delineated ! How rich and luxuriant are the gardens that beautify their sides ! But you cannot see them at any great distance, for the atmosphere is hazy. The people are active in their various occupations, which in the towns we pass are generally divided between gardening and some mechanical employment.

And this is England ! the land about which I have heard and read so much ! It is but a small island, and I remember that when I was a young lad, away in the forest, I often looked at the little spot it occupied on the map, (for geographies had found their way to us), and as I was told it was Great Britain, I inquired, and wondered as I asked, why such a diminutive place should be called "Great." I thought I might put it in my pocket, it looked so portable and insignificant. But now I find it large—not so large in extent of territory as some countries, but large in point of population and the intelligence of the people. Among its inhabitants are some of the most distinguished teachers of the world—men who live their lives in earnest, and who will live in their works for ages.

In this country I see the heart of that commerce whose broad wings are spread over every country in the world. It was here the Anglo-Saxon Race was cradled; here they were educated, and from this place they have gone forth; distinguished wherever they have gone, for enterprise, perseverance and intelligence. These are the qualities which characterize England, and will perpetuate its existence. Its power is concentrated in the intelligence and education of the people, and whatever adds to these will strengthen the bands that bind it, and consolidate the foundation of its government.

But we are now within sight of a great city. The tall black chimneys of its manufactories first attract my notice; then the lofty steeples of its churches; its towering, massive public edifices—all are in view. Stepping from the cars, I tread the streets of the great city of Birmingham.

This is the head of manufactures. The steel which is here made will accomplish the double work of doing good and doing evil—good in the way of subduing the wilderness and causing it to minister to the life of man, and evil in the way of destroying life and making the earth desolate. Implements of husbandry, and the arts on the one hand, and swords, knives, rifles and muskets on the other.

HISTORICAL SKETCH OF BIRMINGHAM.

"Birmingham, a large commercial and manufacturing city, is situated in the north-east corner of Warwickshire. It is seventy-nine miles south-east from Liverpool, and the same distance north-east from Bristol, both in a straight line. As Birmingham is nearly in the centre of England, its situation is elevated. The soil around it is light, but has lately been much improved. The appearance of the city itself is mean; most of the houses being small and of a common class. St. Martins is the only building of great antiquity. Its exterior is rather meagre, having in 1690 been cased with a covering of bricks to prevent it from falling. The spire alone remains in its original state, a graceful monument of olden architecture. The interior is grand and imposing, though disfigured by a coating of plaster and tawdry ornaments. St. Philips church is an elegant building, and, in the opinion of many, forms the chief architectural ornament of the city.

Besides these two, there are ten churches and chapels belonging to the Established Church, and forty-five Dissenting Chapels, several of them elegant erections. Till lately, Birmingham possessed few public buildings worthy of notice, but the citizens are adding to their number. The town-hall is a splendid edifice of Corinthian order, the material being of Anglesea marble. Its length is 166 feet; breadth 104 feet; and height 83 feet. The Saloon, 140 feet long, 65 feet wide, and 65 feet high, contains one of the largest organs in Europe. The grammar-school is a splendid Gothic edifice, designed by Mr. Barry, and erected at an expense of £4000. The theatre, the banks, the libraries, Society of Arts, &c., are worthy of notice. The Schools in Birmingham are numerous and flourishing. Among these may be mentioned the free grammar-school, founded and chartered by Edward VI. Its income derived from land is £300 per annum. The Blue-Coat School, and the Protestant Dissenters' Charity School are supported by subscriptions. There are several associations for moral and intellectual improvement, such as a mechanics' institution, possessing a library of 1200 volumes, the Society of Arts and a philosophical institution. The old library contains about 17,000 volumes, and the new library 4000 volumes. The Savings Bank and provident institutions, and Societies are numerous and highly beneficial. There are also many charitable institutions well supported. The Dispensary, Humane Society, and Magdalen Institution merit great praise. From a very early period Birmingham has been renowned for its manufactures in steel and iron. This trade is now carried on to an extent elsewhere unequalled. The principal branches of it are, plate and plated wares, ornamented steel goods, jewelery, japanery, papier maché, cut glass ornaments, steel-pens, buckles, and buttons, cast-iron articles, guns, steam engines, &c. Birmingham is connected with London and various places by means of canals, and forms a centre of railway communication with every part of the kingdom.

The railway from London to Birmingham, which was opened in 1837, is now amalgamated with the Grand Junction Line, the two forming the London and North Western Railway.

Birmingham returns two members of Parliament. The population in 1831 was 110,914 : including the suburbs 138,252. In 1841 it was 182,922."

Having touched at Birmingham, I am still on my way

to London—now rushing headlong into the base of a hill, where is nothing but darkness, smoke, and noise—now suddenly emerging into light, pleasantness, and joy—and now rushing madly onward as if the old proverb, "Caution is the parent of safety," had been entirely forgotten.

About 2 o'clock, I am in the suburb station of the great city of London. The people swarm like bees, but there is comparatively no confusion among them. The hack drivers are endowed with a most persuasive eloquence, but like certain other orators there is in what they say more sound than sense.

To know where I should go I stood for a while, biting my lips, and leaning on one of the posts. Directly I took a "bee-line" to Mr. Randall's Hotel, in King Street, Cheap-side, where I have been told a great many Americans stay. "What a sight of people!" as one of the New-Englanders would say. Oxford, Holborn and Cheap-side seemed to me literally crammed and suffocating. Old houses, settled at the corners, but looking as if, had they ever been going to fall they would have tumbled long before. Antique and odd-looking edifices, smutty walls, and narrow, worn-out pavements, were among the first objects that presented themselves to my view. And this is London! But I will not speak of it until I have seen something of the city. The famed St. Paul's is but a few steps from here. The General Post Office and the Bank are near by, as well as the fine London Bridge. This is the pasture of John Bull. Here are no signs of French varnish, but "beef and puddings" are plenty.

CHAPTER IX.

LONDON.

My first day in the metropolis must be set down as a ——. Yesterday I did nothing, with the exception of hunting after myself and feeling how strange it was to get lost. The longer I rode, hoping to get from one side of the city to the other, and to attain a position at a distance where I could look on, the more did it seem as if there was no other end to the city.

Following the long, narrow, zigzag course of the streets which met at the door of the Exchange, I had a good opportunity of seeing the most ancient parts of the city.

Here is the reign of noise and confusion. Here commerce centres from all countries; and here are to be seen people from all parts of the world—of every color and name, not excepting the copper-color. Viewing the different parts of the city, I could perceive the gradual change in the style of buildings, which here mark the progress of architecture, and may be taken as a monumental history of this most beautiful of the arts. All the varieties of architecture used by the Britons, from the old-fashioned gables and style of roofing, to the most exquisite compositions of Gothic, Ionic, Corinthian, &c., are to be seen in London. There towers St. Paul's high above the rest, and on account of the smoke of the city looks as if it greeted the sky above the clouds. The General Post Office is a very fine building. Here all day long, including the whole twenty-four hours, can be seen the coaches that convey the letters and papers of the population of the kingdom.

The Postman is a man of importance. His red coat makes him conspicuous, and his employment is not devoid of variety. He sports a whip and a horn. With a blast of the latter he clears the track : to impede his progress would be an insult to the Queen. He feels a great deal *higher* than his Highness the favorite of England, Prince Albert. His red coat covers all defects, in his own estimation, and places him among stars of the first magnitude. Yet of all men he is the most industrious—punctual to a minute in his going and coming—you can always depend on him.

Letters collected from all the surrounding region are gathered into the General Post Office, and from thence are sent to the sub-post-offices in various parts of the city; and so rapidly and methodically does the wheel of this great machine move, that 9 o'clock in the morning brings you letters mailed in Liverpool the evening before, and only a penny a-piece! This cheap postage is perhaps the greatest blessing the British Government has bestowed on its subjects. Whatever fault I may hereafter have occasion to find with the management of government affairs, let me here pay a just tribute to the men who have been instrumental in bringing about this great good. Such a boon should immortalize them; and doubtless it will. This is the great channel of the life-blood of English prosperity, which, flowing in rivulets over the country, will animate the fettered souls of the working classes. By means of the knowledge thus received, they will better their own condition instead of looking to the government with famished eyes for aid. The information they thus obtain will give them the means of living. Neither the failures of the rich nor the perilous times in the crises of commerce, will ever endanger their subsistence. Too much legislation has been always productive of evil. The people stop sowing and reaping to see what government will do, and while resting, the seeds of discord are being sown and a harvest of famine, suffering and death stares them in the face. All lay the consequences at the door of the government, when, if they were rightly viewed, they would be found where they belong—at the doors of the victims themselves.

It is by *teaching* men to *help themselves* that the knowledge diffused among the people will be of more value than the springing of new mines of gold and silver and precious stones. The railroads of England, and the thousands of men who are employed in opening the gateways of light, are doing a great work. Steamboats, railroads, wires—all—all, are urging the "good time coming." The day-star is rising, and the glory it will shed down upon the earth will gladden the homes of poverty. Let it come while I live and stand over the place where the child of Humanity is born, that I may aid in the glad shout, "The world is free, and all nations are happy."

Having delivered several letters on Thursday in the West End, I soon found myself in the company of men whose hearts were endowed with the genuine fire of patriotism and philanthropy. By request of Judge Rushton I went to see the celebrated painter, G., in Kensington, New Town. I found him in his studio—tall, manly, fine looking, and very graceful in his motions. From thence I went to the House of Lords, where I delivered my letters to lord Brougham and others, who cordially received me. They introduced me to the members of the House of Commons. The House was not half full, it being near the close of the session, and many of the members having gone to Scotland on a grouse-shooting excursion.

In going to the House of Commons with Mr. Brown, the member from Liverpool, I expected to see something much more splendid than the Capitol at Washington.

In this I was disappointed, for I had judged of the interior of the building by the grand appearance of the exterior as it stands in bold relief from the Thames river.

The House of Lords is a splendid Hall—full of decorations—stained glass—with symbolic figures—and various designs. The seats are low and without backs; and the roof of the Hall is of glass. There are narrow end galleries, and seats elevated in the end near the door.

The Throne is a large chair gilded with gold. Its decorations are magnificent. The curtains and carpeting most exquisite. I was seated in that part appropriated to distinguished visitors to the country, from whence I could see the few visitors standing near the door. Lord Brougham was then sitting as the chancellor, hearing cases. In the midst of the duties he had to perform he came out first to greet us in the lobby, and ordered the usher to place us in the seat most favorable for observation. I had expected there would be much good speaking;—but to my astonishment there were only two Lords present. On asking why there were not many more, I was told that one could sit and hear all the cases that were to come before the house, and in order to obviate the predicament of speakers in saying "My Lords," (using the plural,) two had to sit, and by their presence justify the appellation. So, thought I to myself, that poor fat man has to sit 7 hours or more to supply the *s* to the word "Lords." This Hall is most gorgeous; yet there is but little comfort either speaking or sitting.

Having gone over the building, which is immense, with Mr. Brown, of the House of Commons, we made an appointment to meet him at his Hotel in the evening when we shall meet more than dozen of the most influential members of the House of Commons, to dine with us.

On repairing to Finton's Hotel, where Mr. Brown stops, we met Mr. Wilson, Commissioner of Government, an M. P. with other Government secretaries, and Mr. Brotherton, the vegetarian M. P. He does not look like the description Sam Slick gives of a vegetarian or Grahamite, when he says he is like a pair of tongs—all legs up to his neck which is small, and his head like a round ball. This Mr. B. is quite another man—so Sam is mistaken for once, though he may be right in the majority of cases.

Many questions were asked me at dinner which I answered as well as I was able. These people know how to live—and well they may, for it has been a great study with them.

CHAPTER X.

ILLUSTRIOUS ILLUSTRATED.

On Monday morning the London News and other papers noticed our presence in the House of Commons on Saturday.

"An Ojibbeway Missionary.—During the sitting of the House of Commons on Saturday, a stranger was observed below the bar, to whom several members paid marked attention. On inquiry, we were informed it was the Rev. George Copway, otherwise Kah-ge-ga-gah-Bow, an American chieftain, who has visited England on his way to attend the Peace Congress at Frankfort. Twelve years ago he was the chief of a tribe of Ojibbeways, and a hunter in the woods; but having visited Illinois during the years 1838 and 1839, he was educated at the expense of some benevolent persons, and baptized, when he returned to his nation, determined to labor for the elevation of the Indian people. Having devised a scheme with that object, he is now seeking the means of carrying it out, and hopes to raise funds in Europe for the purpose. His project is, that the Indians of the northwest, consisting of about 100,000 souls, shall be granted forever about 150 square miles of territory, between the falls of St. Anthony and the west of Minasotah, and by giving them a permanent settlement in this land, induce them to become farmers, and learn the arts of peace and civilization, and it is understood the American government is favorable to the scheme. He is a person of commanding presence, and speaks the English language fluently. During his stay at Liverpool, at which port he arrived in the Niagara, two meetings were held, at which he detailed his plan, but what success is to attend the pecuniary part of it on this side of the Atlantic has yet to be determined."

This week I expect to have a good opportunity of observing the speakers of the House of Commons.

One word about the Hall of this House. It is an ill-proportioned building—constructed, I suppose, according to rules of art, but without reference to comfort or pleasure. The roof is very high, narrow and long—more like a giant coffin than anything else. Benches without backs like the seats of an old-fashioned country school-house.

When this Hall was building the seats were apportioned as follows—Twenty inches were allowed to each member. When they commenced occupying their seats more than one fourth were excluded from the house for the want of room, the corporation of the English being upon the portly order, and ranging above the average dimensions. Some whom I have seen, judging from their portliness, would occupy *two seats* in the House of Commons, for if inches are the measure of a seat which a member is to occupy, the corporeal dimensions of the member himself must add very greatly to his importance.

Monday, at 11 o'clock, we again visited the House of Commons. The speakers were Mr. Smith, one of the secretaries ; Lord John Russell; Bright ; Hume ; Cobden and D'Israeli. The Bill before the House was the yearly appropriation bill for the sustaining and increasing of the Armament of the country.

Here, during the time of each visit, I had a place for hearing and becoming acquainted with the speakers. Baron Rothschild's case came up, the result of which was not in his favor.

At my left he is now sitting—the great banker. His case is now before the House. D'Israeli has just sat down, after delivering a powerful appeal in his favor. They are now debating the Jew Question. Mr. Rothschild has been elected by the people of the city of London. But because he is a Jew they question his right in the House. He cannot subscribe to the oath intended for all protestant members.

His personal appearance is elegant. He moves with ease and grace—no aristocratic air about him—no codfish flavor. In height he is about medium. His hair rather bushy; nose, well formed. While the debate goes on he leans forward and listens with the greatest interest. Occasionally a smile flies over his expressive countenance.

That small man is the man to whom emperors bow the knee as before the God of this world. Only one or two in the House have gone up to him.

Around me are some distinguished individuals of other climes. They have been introduced by some member of the House.

Lord John is a middle-sized person, rather lean, on the Yankee order. His face indicates more energy than physical strength. He is rather quick. His features are short and his nose prominent, a little above the medium size. He leans forward a little when apparently unconscious of it. You naturally attach less dignity to his person than to his mind. He has great penetration, but lacks in power of execution. Yet he will always be valued as a public servant, as one well versed in the past as well as the present political history of his country.

Bright rises, and there is quite a stir in the House. This is in keeping with his noisy, rattling, banging mode of speaking. He speaks well, and is occasionally jovial and sarcastic. His person is rather tall, erect, and borders on the Aldermanic. He is a shrewd politician—one who observes, if he does keep pace with, the progress of the times. He watches the aspects and changes in the political world as some men do the signs and variations in the weather. He dresses plainly and in good taste.

Cobden rises: This is the man whom we in America have found reason to think so much about. Is that Cobden? That one who speaks so hesitatingly and leans forward? There is nothing peculiarly striking in his person. Tall and lean—his face well proportioned—his forehead well formed. Facts, as a certain phrenologist would say, stick out like horns, and with them he does more execution than the graceful delivery and fiery eloquence of many another are able to accomplish. Facts, solid as rocks, are the weapons he uses. The papers which he holds in his left hand are like nails and spikes, and his right hand is like a hammer. His speech is without varnish, but his facts are so ingeniously put forth, one after another, that there is a kind of magic about them; and when in the mind the scale has long gone down, one asks himself, "Why does he still heap up arguments, since he has gained all he desires?" And yet another comes, and another, until you wonder what there is to come next.

Cobden appears to be one of those great men who in the different periods of the world, and in the different countries, have been created by the force of circumstances. He is one who, in my humble opinion, has done a great deal of good, and who will yet be a still greater blessing to his countrymen, and to the world. His overwhelming arguments have rolled over the empire, and echoed among the hills and forests of our own country. His admirers are in every State in the Union. His keen eye sees with a glance the part that should next be enacted on the stage of political life ; and when circumstances favor an explosion of public sentiment, Richard Cobden is there, the champion of the people and the exponent of political rights. Yesterday I heard of a circumstance which heightened my admiration of the man. It was this : During one of the years of agitation with reference to the Corn Laws, the government finding that it could hardly carry its measures through Parliament, it was agreed that Richard Cobden should be offered a situation in the Cabinet as one of its agents in London. The dispatch which was effectually to stop the mouth of the great agitator, was sent. The special messenger having delivered his commission, Cobden was for days all silence. Here was a fat office to secure for life, or for a great part of his lifetime. Principles and pecuniary considerations were at war with each other, and the latter had the honors of office on their side, which in an aristocratic country are not small. The people of England and the powerful government; the hovels of wretchedness and the laurels of State, were arrayed against each other. Night after night and day after day, and not a word from

Cobden. At last *he declines* the honors of State for the good of the whole. Power and wealth cannot buy his principles and his love of his brethren, the laboring classes. He is a promoter of the principles of Peace, of Education, and of everything which makes man worthy of his God.

Next Thursday I take breakfast with him. Many of my friends would wonder, if they knew this, why he should have invited me to breakfast. With gentlemen in England it is the best time to hold conversation with each other, and this makes it a convenient time for him to see me. But I am anticipating.

After the speech of Cobden, another arose, whose name I did not learn, and the bag of wind he discharged reminded me of the man who attempted to propel his vessel in a calm by means of a huge pair of bellows he had placed on board.

Then came the famed protectionist, D'Israeli. The members of the House of Commons pay as much attention to his speeches as the members of the U. S. Senate pay to those of Henry Clay. They gathered around him as soon as he commenced, and on he went with his speech. He is of middle stature, rather thick-set, well-proportioned head, large eyes but not particularly penetrating, with a contour of face uniform rather than otherwise.

He speaks easily but with a great deal of affectation. His gesticulations are few and those very much studied. The winding up of his speech, and the appellation, "my lord," to lord John, to whom he addressed himself, was done with an air of dignity, importance and respect. He has less brilliancy than tact and knowledge of political tactics. Policy is his creed, and he lives up to it. He steps back, is silent for a while, then commences with "My lord"—and all this is for effect.

The personnel of D'Israeli has no doubt aided him in his rise in the House of Parliament. There is always much that is to be admired in the personal history of such men. He like most men who have risen to eminence in political life has gone up upon the stilts of some peculiar circumstance, borne up on the wave of some popular excitement. His power of speech, it cannot be denied, has been a considerable cause of his success. His ability to write is another. A man may be a good speaker, and at the same time a very indifferent writer. To be good in both these capacities he holds a power the strongest of all powers, save the divine.

There is much excitement in the appeals and speeches of D'Israeli, and when he seats himself the applause is almost deafening. I present to my readers a faithful portrait of him from an original sketch.

This morning when I entered the House, I was told that Lord John Russell had just entered, and having seated myself, I inquired which of the crowd was the lord.

" The person sitting next to the pretty Englishman on the left."

" He with a black frock on ?"

" The very one."

He sat there as though he had just turned to allow us a good profile view of his face.

That is the man who has been before the public so long, to see and hear whom the eyes and ears of millions have been engaged. His dress is plain, and without that air and bearing which I thought he had, forming my judgment by what I had read respecting him.

A medium-sized person—lean, yet well proportioned. His face open, his forehead bare and head well formed, with many of its organs very fully developed. His nose rather of the knife order (this is not intended for cutting satire.) His eyes large and piercing, and an index of his disposition. He is easy in his manner, and at home, in every position.

He appears generous to his opponents, and demands like treatment in return.

When he speaks his head inclines somewhat to one side, and his right hand often thrust into the folds of his vest. He attempts no display of oratory. He speaks plain and lays all his arguments and motives open; attempts no concealment of plans, but marks out his course and sticks to it with the tenacity of gold dust to a miser's heart.

One of his Secretaries generally speaks immediately after him, and it is then that Lord John is wide awake. I do not mean to say that he is not at all times "wide awake," but at this juncture he is more than usually so. The restless hands of Hume, Oglethorpe, disturb him.

The satire of D'Israeli, the facts of Cobden, he feels most keenly. They fill his seat with nettles; but he, with a true philosophic mind, admires the ingenious way in which they arrange them, and though they may give pain, he sits on them with *some* satisfaction.

Among the group who have just come to salute me in

D'ISRAELI.

that part of the House which is kindly allotted to me, are some of the most interesting speakers, and Lord John Russell. He comes and seats himself with the rest—the arguments go on; but he does not care the weight of a spike how much may be said by the opposition.

A Leghorn hat is perched upon his head. Now like a school-boy goes and seats himself among the group of his Secretaries.

There is also George Thompson, who was among the first to give us his hand, and welcome us to the floor of the House.

I could faintly remember the sketches I had read of him in the American papers twelve years ago. But not much, for then I was just learning my English alphabet.

A high, well-developed forehead and a Roman nose grace his iron front. He is the friend of the slave. Though I could not subscribe to all his acts and views of employing certain ends for a holy purpose.

I can give you no just idea of his speaking powers—a hurricane is nestling on his brow—and the flashes of fire glow in his eyes. A meat-axe behind his ears. He has a good address, a graceful swing of long arms. and a lion's mercy at the ends of his fingers. I have no doubt he is a smart man by his looks. His full knowledge of this, does him little good. The pronoun *I* is a great stumbling-block to many in this world. To use a common expression they are "*all in my eye.*"

The under-Secretary Smith has just arose to explain. Lord Russell takes things very coolly. He sits on one of the ministerial benches apparently without any concern, and endures all that is said by the opposition with the air of a philosopher.

There is another gentleman just got up to speak—very little hair on his head—quite elderly—tall and as lean as a monument. Why do they laugh? His dress is a good one, as graceful as the rest. "The poor man is the scape-goat of the House," a gentleman whispers in my ears. He stands as firm as a young man of twenty. See, if there is any leaning it is not on the side of old age. In the midst of laughing applause his legs gave way before the cries of his tormentors and the shouts of "go on" from his friends who pity him. I could hardly keep my own tongue still. He said a few words, or attempted to, which amounted to just about nothing or less.

Lord John enjoyed the scene vastly.

This day being quite pleasant there are quite a number of visitors seated in the galleries. Far out some distance from where I sit, I see my friend the Hon. George Folsom, of New York, minister to one of the foreign courts, with his spectacles glistening and looking through them with a vast deal of penetration.

There are quite a number of reporters up in the gallery connected with the various papers. Many of these are now taking notes on which to found some stinging satire for the morrow's papers.

This hall is an ill-constructed thing. It is said that the roof was so high that it had to be lowered in order that the voice might reverberate throughout the house. Before coming here I had in my mind the idea that I was to see something that might have been a model for the Capitol at Washington, or at any rate something superior to it. But I find that it is neither adapted to comfort nor to ease in speaking. The seats are very ordinary, but the decorations are rich and in good taste.

This is the interior of the House of Commons! and now I must go and take a view of it out of doors.

A building of Gothic style, which would cover nearly four squares of New York city There is a great deal of fine work laid out upon it. My friends must imagine they see a tremendous *gingerbread*, nearly a quarter of a mile long, 300 feet high, and 400 wide, and they will have a good conception of its size and looks. The fineness and delicacy of the workmanship will furnish the tooth of Time with a soft morsel.

I gaze with admiration and wonder at the sight before me. From this house will emanate laws that will tell upon the destinies of British subjects throughout the world, and upon the destinies of the race. Before this Hall shall have crumbled into dust, it will have resounded with the eloquence of generations of the greatest and best of the noblest race on the face of the earth. A thousand years hence, the true-hearted Britons will hold on to its tottering walls, and cling to every stone, because those who now occupy it, and the many generations who shall follow, will have made it venerable.

THE NEW HOUSES OF PARLIAMENT.—A parliamentary paper, entitled, " A general statement of the expenditure incurred, and proposed to be incurred, in respect of the site, and in erecting and completing the new palace at Westminster," shows that the total expended for these buildings to be £1,173,240 16*s.* 8*d.*; total unexpended, £824,005 19*s.* 3*d.*; total expended and unexpended, £1,997,246 15*s.* 11*d.*

CHAPTER XI.

RAMBLES IN HAMPTON COURT.

Wednesday morning we set out for Hampton Court, twelve miles from the city—a gay company of select friends. The Solicitor General and ladies of rank are to be with us. This pic-nic has been got up by Mrs. Gibson, the lady of the Hon. Mr. Gibson, M. P.

The country is surpassingly beautiful. Lofty trees hang their branches like arms gracefully by their sides, and beneath their shade the balmy air comes to refresh and cool itself, and to fan the fever from our brows while it causes the social flame to glow more brightly. Here is a glimpse of Eden, with no fiery guard to prohibit us from entering. The garden is well laid out; flowers perfume the air; vines clothe the trees with a green robe sweeping down to the ground; ponds, rivulets, springs and fountains glad the eye; beautiful fish, the goldfish the king of them all, disport themselves in the waters; and there is a group of children at play, their merry shout ringing through the air, and awakening in the breast thoughts of enchanted land and of fairies.

Here are fruits as well as flowers; and now that the latter have closed their eyes and let fall their heads, the former are in demand; for like flowers they gratify taste, and to this they add the gratification of appetite. The evening is beautiful. The heaven within us responds to that without, which is calm and clear and radiant with stars. And there is "Nelly," as they call her, her horns being so well represented in the moon that she forms a part of the scene. In such circumstances we are lively companions, and conspire to make one another happy.

We sailed up and down the Thames—rowed, pulled, and sung. When we had got some distance down the river it began to rain. O mercy!—light dresses, sun-bonnets and summer coats. We were drenched with rain, and before we could get to the house we were bathed in tears wrung out by laughter—such a source of merriment is misfortune!

My friends took something wet inside to dry the outside, and we soon found ourselves in the house again, where we were made comfortable without any inward applications. But we have lost sight of the flowers, and the beautiful lawns with the groups of deer grazing upon them.

Our company being ready we returned to the city. We left the two Misses Marryatt, daughters of the famed Captain Marryatt, behind us. The way was rainy and wet and dark as pitch, until illumined by the lights of the city. Having alighted, entered, seated and warmed ourselves, we were prepared for adventures in dream-land.

This morning, Thursday, at 9½ o'clock, was the time for me to go and breakfast with Cobden. I found him reading papers and letters. He received me cordially, asked me about the country and people, and entertained me with much interesting conversation. Though I had an exalted opinion of him in the first place, he stood much higher in my estimation after this interview. He has a nobler appearance and more urbanity of manners than I expected to find in him, and this was without a particle of affectation. There is no mushroom appearance about him, but a solid English look that I very much admire. We sat together and alone at his table for over an hour, conversing on different subjects. He appeared very conversant with American matters. I will give here a description of him by a hand much more competent than mine.

"Every age produces its own great men, who stand in after times as types of the time in which they lived. Nothing seems so easy as for a great man to be great, and some men have made the mistake of believing that what seems so easy of accomplishment in another, could be accomplished by themselves, and have made wretched failures in their attempts at greatness. Greatness must come naturally, or not at all. Among the men of our own times, who have become great with such apparent ease that it would seem possible for any man to be great who desired it, Richard Cobden, of England, is, perhaps, the most remarkable instance. It is but a very few years since his name was first heard on this side of the Atlantic; in fact, he travelled in this country extensively, took particular note of our morals and manners, yet no one knew that he was in any way more entitled to public attention than any other stranger who visits us for business or pleasure. But if Cobden should come here now, he would be honored with an ovation wherever he might go. He is neither a great orator, a great scholar, a great writer, a great philosopher, a great capitalist, nor a great artist; he is simply a good business man, with great common sense, of humane feelings, and a facile talent of speaking to the middle-men of his country on subjects that appeal directly to their interests.

"Richard Cobden commenced life humbly in one of the manufacturing towns of England, and in time became a partner in an extensive calico-printing establishment in Manchester, where his sign may still be seen, we are informed, over his office-door. When the popular agitation on the subject of the Corn Laws was begun in England, Cobden began to be heard of; he first addressed his own townsmen, and as his reputation spread, he was at last compelled to give up, or neglect his business, while he engaged in advocating the opinions of the Anti-Corn Law League. His popular and forcible manner soon gained him a seat in Parliament, where he distinguished himself by his sturdy advocacy of other reformatory measures; but it was in addressing popular assemblages of the trading and manufacturing classes that he rendered the best service to the cause he espoused, and at last succeeded in procuring the abolition of the Corn-

Laws. The English people, to manifest their gratitude to Cobden, determined to raise by voluntary subscription one hundred thousand pounds sterling, nearly half a million of dollars, and present him. Very nearly that amount was subscribed, with which an estate was purchased that he might be able to devote himself entirely to the public service. He is now member of Parliament for the West Riding of York, and is the foremost man in all the radical movements of the day for reforming governmental abuses and bettering the condition of the people. He ably sustains, in his place in Parliament, every Constitutional measure for republicanizing the Government of Great Britain. Without any of the showy gifts which distinguished such Parliamentary debaters as Sheridan, Fox and Canning, the memory of Cobden is likely to prove sweeter to after generations than either of the brilliant orators named, because it will be associated with acts of beneficence, an untainted moral character, and a reputation for homely goodness which the masses of the people reverence beyond wit or eloquence. Most reformers are men of one idea, but Cobden heartily joins in every scheme that has a tendency to elevate the people and undermine the foundations of aristocratic privilege. He was one of the most active members of the Peace Congress, held in Paris last year, and during the Parliamentary recess, was constantly engaged in addressing the people of his country on the subject of Governmental abuses. If Englishmen enjoyed the blessings of universal suffrage, as it is enjoyed by the people of our free States, the influence of such a man as Cobden would be infinitely greater than it is now. In Parliament he addresses the privileged classes, who are deaf to all arguments that tend to the destruction of the abuses by which they live on the industry of the people.

"Cobden is below the middle height, and of spare habit; one of those men, in short, who Sallust tells us are to be feared in a state. Every syllable he utters is distinct as the organs of speech can make it. He speaks rather slowly at first, and at times somewhat hesitatingly; but this is not because he does not know what to say, but because he is thinking how he shall express his meaning with the very utmost amount of power. He does not seek fine words, but strong ones. And strength there is in what he says, and in his manner of saying it. His sentences are short, like the Roman sword; but they are forged for close warfare and a hard struggle. He

RICHARD COBDEN.

leans forward as he speaks; and with his right arm, as he dashes it downwards, seems to beat his arguments into his hearers' minds. Right or wrong, his whole heart is in the cause. Of that there can be no doubt. He speaks from conviction; and with an earnestness and intensity such as one rarely hears. There is nothing elegant in his language; it is clothed with no ornament, but, like the naked limbs of the gladiator, it trusts entirely to its unaided strength. All he proposes is intelligible; all his reasoning is plain and clear. He knows nothing of theory, but deals solely with facts. He hurls into the arena before you—at your very feet, as it were—some fact, some massive fact; and he tells you to get rid of it—to move it thence if you can. That is his mode of arguing. There is such energy in his manner, such life and energy in his words, that you recognize at once the man calculated to lead in great popular movements, and conduct them to a favorable termination."

I go to Lord Brougham's to dine, at 7 o'clock. Carriages are driving up. Here is Lord ——, Marquis of D——, and Lord F——. This is Sec. —— just returned from a foreign court. A nobler set of Englishmen I never beheld. Lord Brougham, brilliantly dressed, sat at the head of the table. Mr. Gambardilli, the celebrated portrait painter, is there also. He makes a companion of me, and gives me many proofs of friendship.

Lord B., in whatever aspect you view him, has something very remarkable about him. There is nobody like him. In conversation he is fluent and pleasing; two mortal hours and a half over a table. Why, if we had a Yankee here, a green 'un, and he saw us sitting so long at table, he would give us a sermon on Time, with a nasal, I know he would.

Lord Brougham's house is not extravagantly beautiful upon the outside, but the interior is superb.

Next day. A bright, clear morning greeted us. The bustle of the city is not so much felt in the west end, and by the advice of C. F. Dennentt, of Boston, I am pleasantly quartered in George Street, Hanover Square. At a short distance is Regent Street and Park: west of me is Hyde Park; on the south is St. James' Park, and on the south side of this is the palace of the Queen.

This day I visit the Zoological Gardens, to see the Elephant, and more particularly the Hippopotamus, who seems to be the pivot of motion and attraction for the Londoners in dog-days. Dr. W. was to have gone, but we have missed one another. The ride round the Park, and the sight of the trees distributed all about in a picturesque manner, was very pleasant. The elegant mansions, and beautiful public edifices are fitting counterparts of such a scene. This is a charming country, and no wonder an Englishman looks at you as though he felt five inches higher than any man he ever met with. This scenery reminds me of nature's own Parks in the west—those vast openings called Prairies with trees scattered here and there either singly or in clusters.

Here is a world of study and reflection. All kinds of animals from all parts of the world. A mischievous set of the monkey race represents the South, and the white bear, the frozen North—majestic lions—fierce-looking panthers, and a shabby set of grisly bears, have each their iron-bound quarters. Camels looking like a man troubled with rheumatism or gouty gait. Here is the otter—How many recollections of youth it calls up—when I used to hunt them in the woods of Canada. Wolves, foxes, deer—all are here. Among the birds is the Eagle, with his sage-looking head which he seldom turns either to the right or to the left—I seated myself in a chair to contemplate him. There he sat—the monarch of the skies,—how humble now his habitation. The air has been his kingdom, and the sun the goal of his flights. But here you are—what sad reverses of fortune you have experienced! These pale faces are unmerciful to you—never mind, here is *one* that sympathizes with you.

Here are birds of every description and variety of plumage—all kinds of water-fowl, and reptiles.

Here is the Hippopotamus. This animal and the Prince of Naples, who is now in this country, are the two greatest notables just now before the public, but the Prince is, by far, the greatest animal of the two. The one strives to hide his deformity or deficiency of mind under sparkling jewels;—the other stands majestically in his naked, glistening skin. If my friends in America ask me how this animal looks, what shall I tell them? What can I compare him to? He is not like a beaver, though he lives sometimes in the water. He is not a moose, though he stalks about with the same air of dignity. He is not a buffalo, though like him he has a hoof. I have it—I shall tell my people that the hippopotamus looks something like a *fat, shaved Bear*. They must *guess* the rest, or else be content to remain ignorant. See if there is not some truth in my comparison—short clumsy legs—heavy creases in folds about his heels—round plump body—no hair—neck strong—ears short—head large,—mouth, O how big! what in other animals is called a tail, perhaps three and a half inches long, and his color has the appearance of a coating of black lead, with the addition, perhaps, of some soot from the chimney-back.

There is an elephant walking off with half-a-dozen children on his back. His legs look like stumps, yet on he moves with apparent ease. Clumsy as they are, they are of great use to him—and so is his long proboscis. He will do almost anything with it, from hunting nuts in your pocket, to killing a man. Here is an apple. His nose takes hold of it and his nose puts it into his mouth—and the apple is gone.

I might linger here with profit and pleasure all day, yes—several days—but other engagements call me, and I must go.

I find abundance of cards on my table. O fie, fie: these English will spoil me. I have engaged myself for dinner every day this week. My note-book runs thus for the week:

Sabbath morning—go to Mr. Gambardilli. Evening—at Under Secretary's house, Dr. Wiseman to be there. Monday evening—Tea at Mr. S——, New Broad street. Tuesday—Dine at E. Saunders', George Street—a celebrated Dentist. Wednesday—Hampton Court, with Mrs. Gibson's Pic-nic party. Thursday, August 8th—To Breakfast with R. Cobden, at 9 1-2 o'clock. Evening—Dine at Lord Brougham's. Friday—Dine with Lady Franklin and her brother, Sir Simpkinson, 21 Bedford Square.

I have now been in London one week, and have as many more engagements for the next. If I were to go on in this way three or four weeks, I think I should be nearly dead with fatigue.

CHAPTER XII.

ANOTHER VISIT TO LIVERPOOL.

My engagements take me back to Liverpool for a few days, and I must defer the rest of my sight-seeing in London till my return.

Tuesday. I leave the city in company, among others, of a gentleman who seemed to have a very unfavorable opinion of America and Americans—having got most of his information from writers of the Trollope and Dickens' school, of which there are plenty. When he became too personal, I dropped the conversation and took refuge in reading.

Wednesday. I am to deliver a lecture before the Mechanics' Institute on the *Religious belief* of the Indians. Afterwards—another on the superstitions of the Indians and their Legends—and another on the peculiarities of the North American Indians, with their probable

Origin, and other subjects connected with the history of my people in America. These subjects I intend to lay before the British public, both in England and Scotland.

I have sent word that I am going to the Concert of Jenny Lind, after the Lecture, though there is no such thing as buying a ticket—but I have taken it into my head that I will hear her. For several days there has been great excitement in Liverpool about her singing. Even standing room for this concert is said to have been taken long ago. I have seen some ladies and gentlemen who came from Ireland for the sole purpose of hearing her, and others from London.

It is now 7 o'clock, and I must hie to my Lecture. I appear in my Indian costume. To my surprise I find a crowded house, and am received with a kind greeting by my audience.

Here follows the Lecture I delivered :—

Ladies and Gentlemen.—My subject for this evening's lecture is, superstition and legends of the North American Indians. The East is universally allowed by all pale-face writers to have been the birthplace and nursery of superstition, and as I am fully convinced our fathers originated from eastern tribes, to them we owe the great partiality we have invariably displayed for legendary lore and superstitious recitals. The entire traditions of our earliest times, hand down to us but imaginative fables and myths of men and supernatural creatures, changes and extraordinary freaks in the elements, all of which are most strongly tinctured with the ancient Persian philosophy. We do not pretend to establish dates, nor have we any astronomical data, to confirm the exact periods, but we all have a fairy-land location for the first man and woman which we admit a great deluge destroyed. The cause we assign for this event grew out of the following tradition which I will narrate. The name of the hero was Na-nah-boo-shoo. In the latter days of the Old World mankind were numerous, and there likewise were giants and strange half-god monsters who annoyed mankind very much, the animals, some of which were huge and capable of devouring a whole forest tree at a meal, crunching its stem and branches with the ease that a horse masticates his common food, ranged everywhere. Quite as troubled were the waters as the dry land from the stupendous sizes of its creatures. In those days bull-frogs were seen at the least forty feet in bulk, sitting on the banks of rivers, shaking the air by their croakings, like the rumbling and exploding sounds of heavy thunder. The races of men were then much larger than they now are, and fitted with more expansive vitals than those we now know of the greatest size—and human life was in proportion to its dimensions, reaching even the return of a thousand seasons. A very dexterous tribe of hunters were in pursuit of some unwieldy river animals, shooting their arrows indiscriminately amongst a herd who were swimming across a river, when it appears that their flight of missiles exceeded their intentions and accidentally wounded a water-god, whose cries brought speedily about him his whole tribe. They in revenge destroyed nearly all the hunters by hurling huge rocks upon them, and as they did not succeed in the destruction of the whole tribe, they determined to drown mankind. I must now tell you that all the human family were red men then. As the first man was made out of red earth his descendants retained his complexion. Well was it for some of the tribe to have escaped, for they scarcely had reached the mountains near before they beheld the waters gushing up from every direction in the lowlands, thousands of concealed springs became great fountains, playing at least a thousand feet high and deluging all around. Only one man escaped with his wife, and they, having hastily constructed a raft, took with them a few of the smaller animals, such as we now have on it, leaving the larger ones to be, as the red man thought, drowned. The waters rose higher and higher, until the tops of all the loftiest mountains were completely covered. For weeks they floated everywhere, driven by fearful gusts of wind, and exposed to the most terrific action of rain and hail. When this red man, Na-nah-boo-shoo, called out in despair to the Great Spirit and begged for succor, Manitou heard him and put a stop to the great tempests. After some days the red man, not seeing any appearances of land, sent a beaver to dive down in the waters and procure him some of the earth from below, should any be found. The beaver went and after a considerable time had elapsed returned in a most exhausted condition, without being able to find the earth, and died almost as soon as he had got upon the raft. Another was then sent, but it resulted in the same ill success, and he perished from exhaustion. At last a musk-rat was despatched upon the mission, and after a very long time, insomuch that the red man thought he had perished, his little form was seen extended upon his back in the last gasps of life, holding up one of his small paws. He was eagerly rescued from the water and revived with care, when he opened his paw and disclosed that it contained a very small piece of the muddy bottom. This the red man dried carefully, and having reduced it to a powder held it in the palm of his hand, and offering it up with a prayer to Manitou, blew it to the four quarters of the watery waste. No sooner was this done than the tops of the mountains and the upper branches of their trees began to appear, and the waters rushed down through its thousands of subterraneous channels, and off the land to the sea, and the earth was left dry. From this red man and his wife the world was again re-peopled, but with the addition of two other colors,—the pale faces and the black men. From the rapidity with which the world was re-peopled they found it necessary to separate and so branched off, all over the world, to find homes. The red men kept to themselves and found in this country their proper residence. The Manitou, it seems, thought proper to allow some of the giants and huge animals to escape the effects of the flood. It was ascertained that some of them found shelter in the deep caves of that time which existed everywhere, and which they had so secured that no water penetrated. Being friendly with the water-gods, they were preserved partially by their help and food supplied them. These creatures too became numerous and harassed the red men, between whom long wars ensued. The mastodon and the big elk destroyed the lives of many persons. A great-horned serpent next appeared, who, by means of his poisonous breath, produced diseases, and caused the death of many, but the Manitou killed him with thunderbolts. Another calamity was a blazing star which fell in the midst of the red men and destroyed many people. This last event caused them to separate and become distinct tribes, who soon fell into disputes and wars among themselves, which they pursued through a long period, until they utterly destroyed each other's nationality, and so reduced their numbers that their lands were overrun by wild beasts. Those that were left went to a mountain where the Great Spirit preserved them. From the top of this mountain they could behold the sun rise to see him set. They were told that it was heated in great fires below and rose sparkling from them in the morning, cooled off throughout the day, and went down at night to be reheated for the next day's use by the Great Manitou. They all spoke the same language then and resolved amongst themselves to preserve the chain of alliance in such a manner, that no time should be able to extinguish them as one people. They collected together in the West, and divided the country into districts, and these were allotted to Chiefs and Leaders, during the war with the pre-occupying natives, and their descendants are now the various nations of red men.

No people in the world have ever, probably, so completely mingled up their early history in fictions and allegories, types and symbols, as the red men of this continent. Making but little difference between the symbolic and the hostorical, they have left very little distinction to mark the true from the false. Our notions of a Deity, founded, apparently, upon some original truth, is so subtile, and divisible, and establish such a confused admixture of spirit and matter in every shape, that popular belief seems to have entirely confounded the possible with the impossible, and the natural with the supernatural.

> " 'Tis a history
> Handed from ages down; a nurse's tale,
> Which children, open-ey'd and mouth'd, devour;

And thus, as garrulous ignorance relates,
We learn it and believe."

Action so far as respects cause and effect, takes the widest range, through this agency of good or evil influences, which are put in motion alike for noble or ignoble ends, by men, beasts, devils, or gods. The red man beholding some things mysterious and wonderful, believes all are similar, and without the means of navigating his reason, *floats* at fancy's will on a wild sea of foaming and dashing imagination. He beholds a spirit in every phenomenon, and fears a wizard or witch in every enemy. His wild belief in them creates fears and alarms, and terror of the supernatural prompts him wherever he goes to resort to amulet and charm, however ridiculous in themselves, for preservation. A beast, or a bird, a man, god, or devil, a stone, serpent, or a wizard, a wind, sound, or ray of light are so many causes of action vibrating along the mysterious chain connecting earth and skies as it were by telegraphic lines, along which life or death, may at any moment be the reward or penalty of his attention, or disregard.

We were, so say the ancient traditions, long time ago most dreadfully annoyed by the fearful visit of the Flying heads. These heads were enveloped in a beard and hair flaming like fire ; they were of monstrous size, and shot through the air with the velocity of lightning. Human power was not adequate to cope with them. Our priests pronounced them an emanation of some mysterious influence, and it remained with the priests alone, to exorcise them by their arts. Drum, rattle, and incantation, were considered of more avail than arrow or club. One evening, after they had been plagued a long time with this terrific visitation, the Flying head came to the door of a lodge occupied by a single female and her dog. She was sitting composedly before the fire roasting acorns, which, as they became done, she deliberately took from the fire and eat. Amazement seized the Flying head, who put out two huge black paws, from beneath his streaming beard. Supposing the woman to be eating live coals he withdrew, and from that time he came no more among them. The stonish Giants then invaded us. They were a powerful tribe from the wilderness, tall, fierce, and hostile, and resistance to them was vain. They defeated and overcame an army which was sent out against them, and put the whole country in fear. These Giants were not only of prodigious strength, but they were cannibals, devouring men, women, and children in their inroads. Our tradition tells us that these monsters came from the east side of the Mississippi, that existing in forests without habitations, they forgot the rules of humanity ; and began at first to eat raw flesh, and next men. They practised rolling themselves in the sand, and by this means their bodies were covered with hard skin, so that our arrows only rattled against their tough hides, and fell harmless at their feet. Our ancestors finding they could not injure or dismay them fled and hid in caves and glens, and were entirely subdued by these fierce invaders for many winters (or years). At length the great Spirit visited his people, and finding them in such distress He determined to grant them relief, and rid them entirely of these barbarous invaders. To accomplish this he put on the form of one of them, and brandishing a heavy club led them on under the pretence of finding the Mastodon. When they got near the resort of these huge animals, night coming on, he bid them lie down in a hollow, telling them that he would make the attack at daybreak. But at daybreak, he ascended a height, and overwhelmed them with a vast mass of rocks. One only escaped, and he fled towards the north. The huge forms of the rest our traditions tell us are to be seen yet, as the good Spirit killed them.

The belief in Witchcraft prevailed extensively; its effects upon the red man's prosperity and population, according to our traditions, were at times appalling. The theory of the belief was this. The witches and wizards constituted a secret association, and met at night to premeditate mischief, and were bound among themselves to inviolable secrecy. They had power to turn themselves into foxes or wolves, and run swift, emitting flashes of light. They could also transform themselves into a turkey or big owl, and fly very fast. If detected, or hotly pursued, they could change themselves into a stone or rotten log. They sought carefully to procure the venom of snakes or poisonous roots to effect their purposes. They could blow hairs or worms into a person. Once upon a time, say our traditions, there lived a red man near a populous village, who in stepping out of his lodge, to his great surprise, immediately sunk into the earth, and found himself in a large room, surrounded by three hundred witches and wizards. Next morning he went to the council and told the chiefs of this extraordinary occurrence. They asked him if he could identify the persons. He said he could. They then accompanied him on a visit to all the lodges, where he pointed out numbers of them, whom the chiefs put the death-mark on. And before the search finished, a great many of both sexes were killed for belonging to so horrid an association.

A long time back we are told that fifty persons were burned to death at the Onondaga Castle for witches. The delusion prevailed among all the red men. And as late as forty-three years ago, among the Oneidas two females suffered for it. Their executioner was the notorious Hon Yost who figured in the wars of the pale faces about the Revolution. He entered the lodge according to a prior decree of the council, and struck them down with his tomahawk. One was killed in the lodge, the other near the lodge door.

We have a great abundance of stories in relation to fairies, or little beings, so small as scarcely to be visible but to sharp-seeing eyes. They dwell everywhere, and flowers are presumed to shelter large parties of them in a rain shower. The red man as he reclines under the shade of the forests, fancies they are about him; he detects their tiny voices in the insects' hum, and with half-closed eye he beholds them sporting by thousands on a sun-ray. In the evening they are seen and heard, and sometimes revel away the whole night.

" And now they throng the moonlight glade,
Above—below—on every side,
Their little minim forms arrayed
In all the tricksy pomp of fairy pride !"

They are friendly or adverse to him, as he deserves they should be, and great care is taken by him not to offend them. Young Indian girls are often surprised by them and led to their beautiful abodes and shown the wonders of Fairy land. They overhear lovers or disconsolate ones, and aid them as was the case with the Ojibaw maid who loved the Moon. How many years ago tradition does not inform us, but contents itself with handing down to us the fact that on the south-east end of lake Superior lived an old Sachem and his wife who had an only daughter, whose beauty was of so astonishing an order, that her fame spread all through the Indian nations, and many old chiefs sought her father's lodge to obtain the hand of his child for their sons. The young men came in numbers to woo her, but both the old men's petition, and young ones, solicitations were alike displeasing to the young Indian maid, who desired to live single and remain with her parents. Many were the rich offers and inducements made by the warriors around to obtain her. Some went on dangerous expeditions to gain a reputation that she would admire—but that produced no alteration in her mind—she was inflexible. Three of the finest young warriors of her people contended for her, they first went off a war scout and brought her scalps, she heeded them not; they then procured her the most superb offerings of rich furs and feathers, it was useless, she would not even admire them. They then agreed to try their speed before her, if she would let the victor be her companion: she would not consent—they were hopeless. And soon the report spread far and wide of her dangerous beauty, and the side of the Lake upon which she resided, became an avoided spot, lest any of the young braves should see her, and lose their peace of mind forever in love, hopeless, hapless love! During a whole winter, no one came near the lodge of her father: there she remained secluded with her parents, pondering over the heaps of treasure that a host of refused lovers had given her, and endeavoring to recall the best and finest-looking amongst them. A fairy who had watched this fastidious fair one, cast a charm upon her, which immediately produced the contrary effect of her former indifference, and so powerful was it, that it seems she was to fall in love with the first object she should see outside of her father's lodge. And it being night, the first sight that she saw was the moon, which in consequence of the fairy's spell appeared to her as the face of a most enchanting young brave. She sighed and going into the lodge shut the door, and went to rest, but could not sleep, she was so tormented by the love she bore the moon. Early the next morning she took a pail and went to a near spring for water, but forgot what she intended to do, and strolled on some distance along the shores of the lake, lost in admiration of the moon's face. It was the commencement of spring, and the snows had all melted away, leaving the young and tender grass and early flowers in its stead. The birds were about building their nests, and the air was full of sweetness and pleasant sounds. She looked sadly around her, and she saw that every living thing appeared to have a mate. The birds went two and two, the animals the same, and even the tiny delicate flowers appeared to grow up side by side in love and reliance upon each other. Lost in this meditative mood the day imperceptibly to her declined, and the full moon sprang up, to which she turned her looks in desperate emotion of tenderness and love, as she gazed, it seemed to near her, and feeling that she was lifted up from the earth at the same time—she saw that she was hastening to her lover. However, let it be as it may, says the tradition, earth never held her more. And to this day as the Ojibwa braves and damsels behold the shadows upon the moon's face, they imagine they perceive the outline of the fair young Indian maid and her pail.

Our traditions inform us of a huge musquito which infested the lake shores, and destroyed many people. This terrible creature Manitou destroyed, and from his body sprang the present insect of that name. His dimensions were so great that he darkened the country he was flying over.

With tales and traditions of such a kind the Indian beguiles the winter, and the circle around the lodge-fire receives a fresh charm from the horrors and wonderful narrations of its inmates. These stories increase the estimation of home and its safety, for the strong dash of oriental predilection for the marvellous prevails even over the better judgment of the red man—he loves to hear of dangers, when he cannot find them to endure or dare. The spirit of wandering adventure and love of peril forms a striking feature in his own composition.

> "Their dangers and delights are near allies;
> From the same stem the rose and prickle rise."

The forest paths are full of fancy's pictures. Its avenues are enchanted passages, and the whole wood a magnificently adorned palace wherein the red man's heart rejoices. The songs of its gaudy-colored birds are rare music, and the dash of a waterfall nature's accompaniment to the general melody. Here his poetic mind receives its impulses, which the solitudes of the deep woods seem to nurse and cherish. At early morn the dew-sprinkled leaves and flowers exhale delightful odors. At noon when all around is parched, cool breezes seem to assemble in the woods for shelter from the heat. At evening's pensive hour the musical notes of insects awaken, and the night-flowers pour out the fragrance of their incense—

> "Like sweet thoughts that come
> Wing'd from the maiden's fancy, and fly off
> In music to the skies, and then are lost;
> These ever-streaming odors seek the sun
> And fade in the light he scatters."

It would fill folios to recount the many superstitions

in common report among the red men, many of whom to this day truly believe the legends.

In one of the small bays which indent Lake Superior a long time ago, said an old chief, "I have been told there was a small pond, or rather lake, which occupied about some 600 yards of space, being of an oval form. About its margin the wild animals frequented and hither many came to drink—its waters were sweet and wholesome, and the color of it was a deep blue. A great many attempts had been made to ascertain its depth, but so great had been the quantity of line used to no purpose, it was considered by us all as having no bottom. In times past there was an account of its being the abode of a very terrific and formidable creature, which had been repeatedly by straggling hunters, and by one of these I was told about it. He states that being on a scout in search of buffalo, he chose to watch near this place presuming the buffalo would come here to drink about noon—he had hid himself behind a small lump covered with thick bushes, through which he commanded a fair view of the pond. Sometime (after he had waited) he observed the surface of the pond very much agitated, and the water appeared to boil up in a perfect foam; he became uneasy to know the cause, and keeping his eyes fixed on the waters, he soon perceived the form of a huge beast rising from the centre of the lake, which swam towards the shore on the same side with himself. In the meanwhile fear overpowered him, and he was unable to leave his hiding-place from its effects—he saw that this animal was ten times the size of a buffalo, although its head was shaped like that beast and had huge horns on it. Its body was very unwieldy, and its feet were like the bear, armed with monstrous claws. It passed him and rushed off into the woods, when he heard a great outcry of buffalo, some of whom passed his hiding-place in great terror and speed. He continued to watch for the great beast's return, which after a brief space took place. The monster was bloody, and had half a buffalo in its mouth. It came and laid down on the bank of the little lake and finished its meal of raw meat, then sunning itself for an hour, it plunged into the water and began to descend, causing the same agitation to ensue that had characterized its first coming. He saw the impress of the beast's shape on the bank, where it had reclined, and the marks its claws had made in tearing the buffalo. Others came and saw it. And this is believed to refer to the animals' old bones as found in the valleys of the West scattered throughout the country.

Ladies and gentlemen,—I have now only referred to these in an allegorical manner, endeavoring to amuse you more than anything else.—The tales which my brothers in the American forest have preserved, and, like the story of the three black crows, every narrator clips, until it is as black as a real crow.

I must cut my story short for two hours yet, to have the pleasure of seeing and hearing the famed Jenny Lind, and it is now nine o'clock. Thank you for your kind attention, ladies and gentlemen—with a bow.

CHAPTER XIII.

JENNY LIND.

I WAS glad to get through with my lecture, whether my audience was or not. It delayed the pleasure which I anticipated in hearing Jenny Lind for the first time, and therefore I was glad to escape from the sound of my own voice. Whether any of my audience had any other motive in wishing me through, I cannot say. As to my proceedings after my escape from the lecture-room, and my impressions of the songstress, I cannot do better than to give them as expressed in a letter to B. T., of the New-York Tribune.

Liverpool, August 16th, 1850.—I have just heard the identical and far-famed Jenny Lind! An hour ago her voice filled the largest hall that I ever saw—the Philharmonic—containing between four and six thousand people. So great has been the excitement here for these ten days, that everything for sale has Jenny to it. Jenny is in everything—the stores, the sales-rooms, and from the splendid halls to the cellar—all, all things are baptized with the all-potent name of the Swedish young squaw!

"Last week it was said that all the seats had been engaged, and that even the standing stalls were selling at a premium. Not thinking I should be here so long, I had not taken the precaution of previously procuring a ticket; and finding I had to be here on the same evening she sang, yet otherwise engaged, I had to put myself against her singing with a lecture this evening. I had a full house, and immediately cut off my exercises in order to go to the hall to get in. Yes, to *try* to get in! O, presumption; on what will I depend to get in? was a query which had to be solved first. The people who crowded around me seemed to say that I could not, for they had heard that the house was all in a suffocation. Stepping into the carriage, I said, 'I will hear the far-famed Jenny Lind this very night—drive on.'

"Going from the hall where I delivered an address to an infatuated people, I had little time to conclude in what way I had to get in. I had previously, during the day, sent a note saying that the Indian chief would, about nine o'clock, be at the door, and desired a seat if *others had none*, and the hour had already arrived. We drove up. The house was besieged with people. A sea of heads and shoulders! Noise and confusion! 'Who is here!' 'The Indian Chief desires to get admittance,' was the word given by my Arion. 'Come in!' says the man at the gateway, to my astonishment—and as I was stepping out, two of my best friends in this city were by the door, who immediately took me by the hand, and led me by the seats on the aisle—up to the very next from the singers! O! I could hardly credit I was in. The first song had already been sung, and there was an intermission, during which I had the pleasure of being shown all parts of the splendid Hall—and my dress excited as much attention as any one there, for Jenny Lind had not come out then.

"Soon the company of the society began to arrange themselves—and the people settled. One or two pieces were sung, and then came on the sight which my very black eyes were aching to see. The last sound of the chiming of an immense crowd subsided; all eyes turned toward the door of the closet where she was, and so soon as the door opened, cheers, deafening cheers, filled the

Hall! clapping of hands! waving of handkerchiefs by the ladies all over the house! yet still I was not moved. She bowed a most exquisite, modest bow!—Her dress quite plain, yet gracefully made. Her hair—no profusion of flowers, nor the wild extravagant torture of the hair. Her form is slender—a full chest—and a mouth like that of the Hon. Henry Clay. She glanced her blue eyes over the sea of heads. Her eyes sparkled like stars glimmering in a cloudless sky. Her motions were easy and natural. She sang. Her very first notes thrilled through me. The immense house full of people were in agony at some of her touching notes. O, what unearthly and heavenly music! My soul, wrapt in ecstacy, seemed borne on to the Garden of Eden. I could appreciate the poet's words:—

> "'—— Her deep and thrilling song
> Seemed with its piercing melody to reach
> The soul, and in mysterious unison,
> Blend with all thoughts of gentleness and love.'

"Her voice echoed all over the house. Then arose the maddening shout; for a minute they cheered to get her back! Sure enough she came, and sung over the same piece and then retired. I then could breathe freer, for I had been holding my breath with intense interest while she sang.

"A lady by my side sat motionless, like a statue, yet the tears sparkled as they wound their way on her cheek with her breast heaving with emotion. Another, and yet quite an aged gentleman, gazed with interest, the perspiration rolling down his face ; he turns to his lady and says : 'She sings like our poor Emma used to, before she died.' Both wept.

"Oh ! tell the poor classes all over the land, that this far-famed vocalist was once an obscure girl—yes, a poor girl. Let them imitate such examples, and be something while they live.

* * * * * *

* * * * * *

"Yours, truly,

"KAH-GE-GA-GAH-BOWH."

CHAPTER XIV.

BAPTIST NOEL—TRAVELS TO COLOGNE.

THIS evening I delivered another lecture before a good house; and at a quarter after nine o'clock I leave for London again, travelling all night. Here I leave my lady until I return from Germany.

The night was tedious, and though I am capable of sleeping soundly in almost any situation, I awoke several times before getting to the London station. I have here to get myself ready, for on Monday I leave for Frankfort on the Main.

I arrived in London about 4 o'clock, and felt about as bad as I looked: Again I quartered myself in George street, Hanover square, where I saw several gentlemen from America, travelling and enjoying the strange sights of the Old World. A Mr. K., from New York, is the life of our company. He runs down the English and makes fun of their peculiarities, "just for greens," as we say in the west.

Sabbath morning. This is a beautiful day, and the sky is very clear for England, for here we see the sun about once a week, and that only for a few minutes. The streets are comparatively still, and the people are going to church. I lay out to go and hear the great and pious good man, the Rev. Baptist Noel, this evening, for I cannot be content with hearsay—I must go and hear for myself.

The night coming on, we repaired to an old Chapel in the north part of Oxford street. The building is very simple, no decorations, the seats or pews high-backed and plain, without cushions. The pulpit projects from the wall, in the old-fashioned style. The people began to come in, and soon the aisle and every part of the house was filled. I was seated about half-way up the aisle in a good seat, and in a favorable position to see and hear.

The door of the vestry opens, and forth he comes, and kneels down on the cushion at the Bible desk. Now we see him to advantage. His kneeling form incites to the same posture in the observer, for it bespeaks the posture of the mind. The reader commences. O, wretched!

He sings it out in a monotonous tone, varied only by a twang that serves to fix the attention, not to the reading, but to the manner of it. What is still worse and more absurd, he reads with an air, as though he were delighted with his performance. The *genuine* singing is then gone through with, and at the close the Reverend man prays. Stillness reigns throughout the house. I never felt before how a man could talk with God!—so fervent, so humble, so simple—such saint-like simplicity! His trembling and faltering voice vibrates along the galleries with a heavenly sweetness that seemed to dissolve into the whispering of angels. The cause of humanity escapes not his prayer. He calls down blessings upon his audience. Individuals, even, are held up one by one, and the tender language of love and sympathy falls from his lips, and springs in an overflowing fountain from his eyes, and rolls in drops along his earnest face.

I loved the man before, but I love him better now. I love all things which discover the better nature in man, which stir the depths of sympathy, and which give evidence of the living soul that was breathed into man at the creation. O, could men have more of this and less of self, I would be willing to spend an eternity of years in this world. But self-love makes a hell for mankind, and with this they torment each other.

Having ended his prayer, the pastor rose and read, and it was the sense you listened to as well as the language and manner. He is tall, leans forward a little—his face is neither full nor lean, the forehead is well developed, his arms are long; and as to his eloquence, when he had spoken about twenty minutes, I said to myself, "Can this be Baptist Noel?" for, for plainness I never did hear any one to equal him! A child might easily understand him. A man of ordinary capacity might preach as good a sermon, if not better, so far as talent is concerned. What then is the peculiarity of this man's discourse which distinguishes him? It is simplicity, fervor and love. There are here, no flights of oratory, no distortion of countenance, no awkward display of ungraceful arms.

His discourse was long, yet none moved from their seats. The audience followed him from beginning to end. After presenting the sweetness and holy character of our Lord, he turns to the sinner with a look that I never shall forget. "This is the Saviour whom you despise."

So much of deep compassion his face reveals that the

people partook of his feelings, yet could not respond. The audience could but weep. In the interval following that sentence I thought angels could have looked down with wonder and admiration, yea, with tenderness and sympathy.

On he goes, in still sweeter strains, praising and glorifying his Redeemer, and expressing his solicitude for the eternal welfare of the vast assemblage.

As he closed his long and faithful sermon he offered a prayer, to which I could respond with a swelling heart, *Amen.*

The breathless stillness is broken. The clerk again makes his rehearsal, a sound of unintelligible words.

I was requested to see him in the vestry, and assenting gladly, there found him the same warm-hearted, earnest preacher.

We bid him adieu. As I stepped out my thoughts recurred to men of renown whom I have seen. Men who in the world's estimation are esteemed "great." But I had just seen a greater than they. I felt like a child, and would have wept, an hour, yea, a day, to have tarried with him. I may have the pleasure of enjoying an eternity with him.

This is the man who lately caused no small sensation in the Established Church by his arguments in favor of baptism by immersion. I find in conversation with Episcopalians that many of them still esteem him very highly for his benevolence of heart and his true piety.

Weary and tired I lay me down, desirous of gaining some rest, as to-morrow I must leave with the delegation from London for Frankfort-on-the-Main.

This morning (August 19th) we have beautiful weather, and the prospect of a very fine day.

Having seen a few friends, I now leave. It will take one hour to pick out my hazardous way amid omnibuses, hacks, stages and go-carts.

I need not speak of the disappointment experienced so often by pedestrians in the great city of London. Those who have been there will at once chide me for allotting so short a time as one hour for my undertaking.

Here I am with my trunk and carriage blockaded by any number of drays, 'busses and so forth, et cetera, completely pent in, as a ship by icebergs, with no chance to go this side or that, on or back.

Hark! how the pugnacious drivers talk! they swear like troopers, though I never heard troopers swear, yet I know they couldn't do it worse. And while I am waiting they are swearing over their horses' backs. My watch says IV. yet I'm not in sight of the bridge.

"Driver, go on, do propel, and you shall have 2*s*.6*d*. more. Do get to the station before the train leaves."

My friend Dr. Francis of New York sometimes styled me a P———r, but here it tried my patience and good temper very severely.

"Is the train gone?"

"No, they are soon going—bless them."

"Are you going to Frankfort?"

"Yes, sir."

"Let me see your card."

Peace Congress,

FRANKFORT ON THE MAINE.

No. 227. [VIGNETTE.] DELEGATE.

GLORY TO GOD IN THE HIGHEST; ON EARTH

PEACE.

REV. GEO. COPWAY.

Departure from London Bridge Station,
Monday, Aug. 19th, at 4 in the afternoon.
Sittings of Congress, Aug. 22, 224.3,
Departure from Frankfort on return on the
morning of Thursday, Aug. 29.

WILLIAM STOKES, SECRETARY.

"Pass in."

"Hurry, hurry, my man." I have my seat safe; my trunk also, and about me is a set of jovial, hearty Englishmen with a sprinkling of lean Yankees.

At quarter-past four our conductor whistles, and at the signal more than sixteen cars are drawn out, all crowded full, for there are over five hundred in the company, though a great many have gone on in previous trains, and will meet us in Frankfort.

The scenery along the railway is very beautiful, rolling hills dotted with trees, and valleys filled with harvesting, farms well cultivated, trees and shrubbery growing, and industrious people working.

But as we pass everybody looks at our train, wondering.

Dover—the place of our embarkation. We have been running through deep tunnels, going, really, by faith and not by sight. We are now stepping on board a swift steamer, for Calais.

The light-house is in view. The wind blows fierce, the waves rise high, and the channel is in a foam. Beneath the beautiful rays of the moon how brightly the waters glisten. And how our boat plunges amid the waves. It begins to toss about. The ladies begin to lie down. It matters not where, for Old Neptune is giving them a shake, so the floor is better than no place.

Sea-sickness! awful pleasure!

What an internal improvement is progressing. It seems as though the committee of interior had ordered a search for smuggled goods, fearing that from England we might carry over some hardware in our stomachs, to France, and neglect to pay duty.

The saloon is packed with prostrate passengers. Some sick, very sick, and angry with the Captain because he will not stop and let them get out!

Gentlemen stand on the deck, doing all they can to keep themselves down, and their meals, ditto.

We who are well, cannot but smile at the very ludicrous figure which some make, but the pitiful looks of ladies, and the desponding looks of gentlemen, seem to say, "We don't see anything to *laugh* at."

A few moments pass, and we are in the harbor of Calais, just before us is the first of Brother Crapeau's land.

A beautiful station is it, and just at the river's side.

Now, it is French, French, French. Nothing but French. Nothing than French. Nothing except French. Here we are taking *la coffee.*

The people here seem to have made calculations as to how much money they would make by us; no very small sum neither. Exchange Officer is here, and those who have a delegation ticket, are allowed to pass their baggage over without much trouble

A little after eleven o'clock, at night. We are now ready, and our conductor blows a blast of his horn, which has the same signification as the "whistle" of the Englishman, and the "all aboard" of the Yankee.

But here, before I leave Calais, I will give you some historical reminiscences of the place.

"Calais has 10,000 inhabitants; it is a fortress of the 2d class, situated in a most barren and unpicturesque district, with sandhills raised by the wind and the sea on the one side, and morasses on the other, contributing considerably to its military strength, but by no means to the beauty of its position. An English traveller of the time of James I., described it as 'a beggarly, extorting town; monstrous dear and sluttish.' In the opinion of many, this description holds good down to the present time.

Except to an Englishman setting his foot for the first time on the Continent, to whom *everything* is novel, Calais has little that is remarkable to show. After an hour or two it becomes tiresome, and a traveller will do well to quit it as soon as he has cleared his baggage from the custom-house, and procured the signature of the police to his passport, which, if he be pressed for time, will be done almost at any hour of the day or night, so as not to delay his departure. It is necessary to be aware of this, as the commissionaires of the hotels will sometimes endeavor to detain a stranger, under pretence of not being able to get his passport signed.

Travellers landing at a French port, and not intending to go to Paris, but merely passing through the country, as on the route to Ostend or Brussels, are not compelled to exchange their passport for a passe provisoire, but merely require the visé of the authorities at Calais to allow them to proceed on their journey. Persons unprovided with a passport, may procure one from the British Consul for 4*s*. 6*d*.

The Pier of Calais is an agreeable promenade, nearly 3-4 of a mile long. It is decorated with a pillar, raised to commemorate the return of Louis XVIII. to France, which originally bore this inscription :—

'Le 24 Avril, 1814, S. M. Louis XVIII. débarqua vis-à-vis de cette colonne, et fut enfin rendu a l'amour des Français ; pour en perpétuer le souvenir, la ville de Calais a élevé ce monument.'

No one needs to be reminded of the interesting incidents of the siege of Calais by Edward III., which lasted 11 months, and of the heroic devotion of Eustace de St. Pierre and his five companions. Few, however, are aware that the heroes of Calais not only went unrewarded by their own king and countrymen, but were compelled to beg their bread in misery through France. Calais remained in the hands of the English more than 200 years, from 1347 to 1558, when it was taken by the Duke de Guise. It was the last relic of the Gallic dominions of the Plantagenets, which, at one time, comprehended the half of France. Calais was dear to the English as the prize of the valor of their forefathers, rather than from any real value it possessed."

This town is perhaps Anglicized in great measure as it is by the proximity of Dover, and the English dominions. There are a great many people here from England, some for trade, others for different purposes. The historical associations of this place are numerous.

The ruins of old fortifications, and the vestiges of war, it is said, have destroyed this place of associations.

Lady Hamilton is buried in the outer skirts of the town, where, it is said, she died in utter want.

The night is cold, and we are going over a very level country. Group after group of houses, we pass. And the country presents in the night more monotony than in a waste of plain like the Prairie of the West. Our company though numerous are all still, bowing in the dark, and a great deal more polite than they are when wide awake, for it is all *self* here. Not so much attention to one another. This might be tolerated by an American if this only existed among the men. But, a lady here, so far in my observation, receives no more favors on account of her gentleness, and I might say helplessness in travelling alone.

Whatever it may be in the American, whether a mere love to show off or a desire to please in the attentions which are paid to ladies in America in general, a thing which is commendable in them. The creed with most men well bred seems to be—"Be civil to all, since in doing so it neither takes any of ours nor the qualities you possess." Which is by far the best than this growling, and snarling, at everything which does not exactly meet one's approbation.

I have seen a want of decorous action in men, here in England, which I certainly did not expect to have found before I left from my native land. It is true that at times ladies by their over-abundance of impudence do not deserve a fair treatment; yet still they plead they are the "weaker and gentler sex," and ought to be treated accordingly.

Enough of this, for we don't travel here to moralize on the present, as we may do at some other time. Yet, still I will abuse no one. Even if a man is too mean to be noticed, I would not have his name in the routine of names now dear to my heart among the English.

We are coming to some place. Stopped but once since we left.

A town which is called St. Omer.

It is described as a fortified town in a marshy situation, with 21,000 inhabitants.

"The Cathedral is a fine Gothic building, containing many interesting relics from the once celebrated city of Terouanne, but heavy and stunted in its proportions. The tower, porch, and interior are most worthy of observation. The most remarkable building, however, is

The Church of St. Bertin, destroyed in the revolution :

it exists now only as a most beautiful and interesting ruin; but it is to be feared that it may not long remain even in this state. It was once considered the finest ecclesiastical edifice in French Flanders; equally distinguished for size, purity, and uniformity of style. It afforded an asylum to Thomas à Becket while banished from England. The choir was finished in 1353, the transepts in 1447; the nave and tower, begun in 1431, were not completed till 1520, two centuries after the commencement of the edifice. At the revolution the abbey was suppressed, and its property confiscated. The church, which had been spared by the Convention, was sold under the Directory, and demolished, in 1799, for the sake of the glass, metal, and wood, which were disposed of in lots. Since that time the ruins have suffered much from exposure to the weather; and nearly all that remains of the nave and transepts is likely to perish in a few years: but the tower is almost perfect, with the exception of the mullions of the windows, and with the assistance of some walls built across the openings to support it, may be prevented from falling.

A Seminary for the education of English and Irish Catholics exists here: it has succeeded the celebrated

Jesuits' College founded by Father Parsons for the education of young Englishmen. Daniel O'Connell was brought up here for the priesthood, and several of the conspirators engaged in the Gunpowder Plot were pupils of the same school. There are not more than 15 or 20 students at present."

Just at daylight after leaving this place, we had a short time to rub the dust from our eyes and to look at the country of the Belgians. This is a monotonous country—no hills to see. But one continual level of mud and stagnant pools of water. A very easy country to grade railroads, and a fine country for farming if it was not so level. These people seem to be very industrious. Women are as often seen in the fields as men, substantial they are too. Firm, and rugged-looking faces as round as the fat face of the moon.

Towards 9 o'clock, we have not got any breakfast yet, and I feel as though I could devour any kind of eatable substance. We now come to Lille, and I am too busy in attending to my bodily wants then to rake any historical notices of the place. The people are busy looking at us, and they certainly must wonder when they see us eat, if this is the way we devour our food, where we come from. Some of us do not do so, and others of us worse.

This morning to philosophize over a cup of coffee had to be dispensed with. For none seem to have manners enough left, to help the others.

The town is described as a city of importance, with 70,000 inhabitants; handsomely built, and surrounded by fortifications which render it one of the strongest places in France. Its citadel is considered a masterpiece of the skill of Vauban, who was governor of it for many years. At different periods, and under different masters, Lille has stood seven distinct sieges; the most memorable, perhaps, was that by the allied armies of Marlborough and Eugene in 1708, of three months' duration, during which the war was not merely waged above ground, but the most bloody combats were fought below the surface between the miners of the opposite armies, each endeavoring to sap and undermine the galleries of his opponent.

Boufflers, the French commander, after a masterly defence, was compelled to capitulate, but upon the most honorable terms.

The Rue Royale is a fine street nearly a mile long

The most interesting public buildings are the ancient Hôtel de Ville, built by Philip the Good, 1430, and the Cathedral of St. Maurice, in which the Duke de Berri was buried. Its exterior is utterly uninteresting : the interior is good, and worth seeing.

The Public Library of 20,000 vols. is a remarkably fine collection, and contains, besides, a number of very curious MSS. charters, &c.

In the Church of St. Catherine there is a very capital picture by Rubens,—the Martyrdom of St. Catherine; but hung so far above the high altar that it can with difficulty be seen.

The Museum of Natural History is rich in the birds, fishes, insects, and minerals of the surrounding district.

There is a handsome Promenade and a tolerable Theatre here.

Lille contains little to detain a traveller not interested in manufactures, but so much active industry as is visible here is rarely found in a fortified town; it possesses 150 cotton factories, which have risen up in the room of the manufacture of lace, for which it was once famous. It has, besides, numerous other important manufactures; and its trade and commercial prosperity are much promoted by the two navigable canals which traverse the town. The cultivation of beet-root for sugar is carried on to a great extent in the country round Lille.

Outside the Paris gate are nearly 200 windmills, principally used for grinding rapeseed.

There are not so many curiosities in this town as to pay any man for seeing and visiting. The streets are old-fashioned and houses ancient. Mud-walls falling in pieces —signs of houses very prominent.

At a little after 10, we are here in Ghent, celebrated for its many curiosities and ancient buildings. No town seems to possess that claim of attention as this does. But, we cannot even go up to the streets to see it, for we stay but 10 minutes. There are in sight, many public buildings. The curious roofed and gabled houses, high, painted roofs, and curious devices around them strike my eye. The grass is literally covered with drapery goods and cottons, bleaching.

Long before we came to it did we see its steeples. Being a clear morning, the sky is fine, and the atmosphere bracing.

Our company is gathering, and we will soon be on our way again. This city is associated with many stirring events. To Americans more than any city in this kingdom.

The following are a few of the historical associations connected with this city.

Ghent lies upon the rivers Scheldt and Lys, whose numerous branches, traversing the town, form canals in all directions: it has about 92,000 inhabitants. In the time of Charles V. this was, perhaps, the largest and most populous city of Europe. It contained 35,000 houses, and 175,000 inhabitants; and that emperor used sportively to say that he could put all Paris into his glove (gant). The circumference of its walls at the present day measures between 7 and 8 miles. In the 10th century it was the capital of Flanders, but in process of time the turbulent weavers, among whom a spirit of independence had early begun to work, rose up against their feudal superiors, and threw off their yoke, or obtained from them concessions and immunities which formed the origin of popular rights in Europe. At length its burghers became so bold and warlike, that they were able to repulse from their walls 24,000 English, commanded by Edward I., in 1297; and contributed to beat the *élite* of the French chivalry at Courtray, in the "Battle of

Spurs.' Their allegiance both to the counts of Flanders and dukes of Burgundy, seems to have been little more than nominal; since, whenever these seigneurs attempted to impose a tax which was unpopular, the great bell sounded the alarm, the citizens flew to arms, and slew or expelled from the town the officers appointed by their sovereign. It did not take long to equip an armament of burghers and artisans, who had weapons always at hand, and who repaired to the scene of action in their every-day or working dress, only distinguished by a badge, such as a white sleeve worn over it, or a white hood. Thus it happened that popular tumults were as frequent in the 14th and 15th centuries in Ghent as they have been at Paris in the 19th, and rather more difficult to quell. On the other hand, it not unfrequently happened, that the seigneur, aroused by some act of atrocity or insubordination, collected his forces together and took signal and terrible vengeance. These courageous but undisciplined citizens then atoned for their audacity on the field of battle, being mowed down in thousands. Afterwards came the season of retribution and humiliation for the town: enormous subsidies were levied on it; its dearest privileges were confiscated; and its most honored citizens and magistrates were condemned to march out of the gates in their skirts, with halters round their necks, and to kiss the dust before the feet of their imperious lord and conqueror. The city of Ghent was several times forced to make such an abject and ludicrous act of submission. The immediate cause of its decline and ruin may be traced to this spirit of revolt. "Intoxicated with the extent of their riches, and the fulness of their freedom," the citizens engaged in a contest with their sovereign, Philip the Good. It is no little proof of their vast resources that they were able to maintain it from 1448 to 1453; but in the end they were compelled to submit, with abject humiliation, heavy fines, and loss of trade.

In 1400 the city of Ghent is said to have contained 80,000 men capable of bearing arms. The number of weavers then amounted to 40,000; and they alone could furnish 18,000 fighting men out of their corporation. A custom derived from that period still exists in the town:— A bell was rung at morning, noon, and evening, to summon the weavers to their work and meals; while it tolled, the drawbridges over the canals could not be raised for the passage of vessels; and other persons were even enjoined not to go out into the streets, for fear of interrupting the vast stream of population; while children were carefully kept within doors, lest they should be trodden under foot by the passing multitude.

Though fallen from its high estate, and sunk both in population and extent of manufacture below what it was in the proud days of Burgundian rule, it does not display the same signs of decay and listlessness as Bruges: it is still the *Belgic Manchester*. In 1804, while united to France, it was ranked by Napoleon as the third manufacturing town in his dominions, after Lyons and Rouen. The revolution of 1830, however, has inflicted another vital blow on its prosperity; and there are now many workmen out of employ. Several considerable manufactures are carried on here, especially that of cotton. In 1801, a clever Fleming, named Lieven Bauens, brought over from Manchester English workmen and spinning-jennies. The manufacture quickly took root, so as to employ in a few years more than 30,000 workmen. Sixty steam-engines were employed, not long ago, in the town and neighborhood to set in motion the machinery of the various cotton mills. But since the Revolution many have ceased to work, and several proprietors have removed their establishments to Holland.

The picturesqueness of the houses of Ghent, the fantastic variety of gable ends rising stepwise, or ornamented with scrolls and carving, arrest the stranger's eye at every turn."

No country that ever I visited possesses such sameness as this. Nothing seems to be anywhere, which could give it the contrast. All alike, the land is cultivated. The group of willows, and rows of poplar trees, are the principal objects which are seen along the flat road. Some places the farms are so immersed in water that they appear more like lakes skirted with wood. Women are useful here. They are up to the knees in mud, digging up or fishing up their potatoes—fine fields of this useful article of food are now covered with water. They appear to be devoid of curiosity, for when our trains are passing, they do not even look to see the train as it whizzes by them. Working away without any interruption. Tobacco is grown here for each farm, as one corner of it may be seen growing.

The road is very dusty. We soon will get to the frontier of Belgium.

The next place of note we come to is Liége. It is situated where, around it are mountains the first of the kind we saw. The scenery is fine around it, being down somewhat in a valley. The following are some of its historical associations:

"Liége lies at the junction of the Ourthe with the Meuse; it has 58,500 inhabitants, and differs from most other Belgian towns, inasmuch as it at least appears to be thriving. The clouds of smoke usually seen from a distance hanging over it, proclaim the manufacturing city, the Birmingham of the Low Countries; and the dirty houses, murky atmosphere, and coal-stained streets, are the natural consequence of the branch of industry in which its inhabitants are engaged. The staple manufactory is that of fire-arms; Liége is, in fact, one great armory, and produces a better article, it is said, at a low price, than can be made for the same sum in England. The saddlery is also very good here, and a particular kind of coarse cloth is manufactured in large quantities. There is a Royal Cannon Foundry here, and Mr. Cockerill manufactures spinning machinery and steam-engines to rival the English. The cause of this commercial prosperity is, as might be conjectured, the presence of coal in great abundance close at hand. The mines are worked upon the most scientific principles: some of them are situated so near to the town that their galleries are carried under the streets, so that many of the houses, and even the bed of the river, are in some places undermined. Previous to the Revolution, Holland was supplied with coal from Belgium; but the home consumption has since increased to such an extent, from the numerous manufactories which have sprung up on all sides, that the Belgian mines are now inadequate to supply the demand, and a law has been passed permitting the importation of coals from Newcastle.

The buildings best worth notice in Liége are, the Church of St. Jaques and the interior court of the Palais de Justice, formerly palace of the Prince Bishop, built by the Cardinal Bishop Erard de la Marck, 1533. The stunted pillars of the colonnade which surrounds it bear a resemblance to those of the ducal palace at Venice, and have a striking effect with much the same character as those found in works of Moorish architecture. Each pillar is carved with a different pattern.

A visit to Liége, and the mention of the Bishop and his palace, are likely to call to the mind of an Englishman the vivid scenes and descriptions of Quentin Durward. He will, however, in vain endeavor to identify many of the places there spoken of, with the spot. The Bishop's "Castle of Schonwaldt, situated about 10 miles from the town," cannot be Seraing, as it was not built till a much later period. Sir Walter Scott never visited Liége himself, so that his localities are purely imaginary; yet, from the vividness of his description of the town, and the perfect consistency of all his topographical details, few readers would doubt that he was personally acquainted with it. He has also made a slight variation in the romance from the real facts of history as far as relates to Liége: and as the events on which he founded the novel are of the highest interest, and serve to illustrate the story of this ancient "Imperial free city," it may not be amiss shortly to relate them. The citizens of Liége, puffed up, as Philip de Commines says, by pride and riches, gave constant proofs of their boldness and independence by acts of insubordination, and even of open rebellion against their liege Lord, Charles the Bold of Burgundy, and against the bishops who were his allies or supported by him. He had inflicted severe chastisement upon the Liégois after his victory at St. Trond (when many thousands were left dead on the field), by abridging their privileges and taking away their banners; and when they submissively brought him the keys of the town, he refused to enter by the gates, but compelled them to batter down the city wall for a distance of 20 fathoms, and fill up the ditch. He then entered by the breach, with his visor down, his lance in rest, at the head of his armed bands, as a conqueror ; and further, to disable the bold burghers from mutiny, ordered all their fortifications to be demolished. This punishment was inflicted in 1467, but it was so little regarded, that the very next year they again broke out into open revolt, at the instigation of secret emissaries of Louis XI., seized upon the person of their bishop in his castle at Tongres, and brought him prisoner to Liége.

They were headed by one John de Vilde, or Ville, called by the French Le Sauvage : it is not improbable that he was an Englishman, whose real name was *Wild*, and that he was one of those lawless soldiers who at that time served wherever they got best paid, changing sides whenever it suited them."

Immediately after we left the frontier of Prussia in Belgium, we came to the Rhenish Prussia ; and we have just stopped 10 minutes in Aix-la-Chapelle. This to me is a very interesting place on account of its many historical reminiscences.

"Aix-la-Chapelle, a town of 37,800 inhabitants, was known to the Romans under the name of Aquis Grani. The warm springs were a sufficient inducement to fix that bath-loving people on the spot, and remains of their baths are constantly found in digging. It is to Charlemagne, however, that the city owed its eminence. He was born here, as some conjecture, and without doubt died here, 814. He raised it to the rank of second city in his Empire, and made it capital of his dominions N. of the Alps, appointing it the place of coronation for the German Emperors his successors.

In the middle ages it flourished with the privileges of a Free Imperial City, and attained great eminence in its manufactures, especially in that of cloth, for which it is celebrated, even to the present day.

In later times it has been distinguished by the Congresses held here—1. In 1668, when a treaty of peace was concluded between France and Spain ;—2. In 1748, when a general peace was signed by the sovereigns of Europe ; and—3. In 1818, at which the Emperors of Austria and Russia, and the King of Prussia, were present in person, and Ambassadors were sent from George IV. and Louis XVIII. to decide on the evacuation of France by the Allied armies.

After the peace of Paris, Aix was separated from France, to which it had been united by Napoleon, and added to the dominions of the King of Prussia. By the handsome new streets and fine buildings erected since that event, as well as by the increase of population, it appears to be returning to its ancient prosperity. Since the days of the Romans and Charlemagne, it has been celebrated as a watering-place, and is annually frequented by many thousand visitors.

The Hôtel de Ville (Rathhaus), in the great market-place, is a vast and somewhat imposing building. Strangers generally become acquainted with it when they repair thither to have their passports signed in the Police Office, situated in the right wing, near a small tower, said erroneously to be of Roman origin, and called the Tower of Granus. The Rathhaus occupies the site of the palace in which Charlemagne was born; it is remarkable as the place of meeting of the two Congresses of 1748 and 1818. In the grand saloon on the second floor, where the conferences are held, are shown some bad pictures of the members of the congress collectively, and some equally bad portraits of the ministers and sovereigns who assisted at them; among them, that of Lord Sandwich, the English minister, is conspicuous. The smaller room on the same floor was occupied by Sir Thomas Lawrence as a painting-room in 1818, while painting the portraits of the sovereigns and other eminent persons then assembled, for the gallery at Windsor.

In the centre of the square is a fountain, surmounted by the bronze statue of the Emperor Charlemagne. It appears to have been erected at the same time as the Rathhaus, in 1353.

The position of the Tomb, in which once reposed the mortal remains of Charlemagne, is marked by a large slab of marble under the centre of the dome, inscribed with the words, "CAROLO MAGNO." A massive brazen chandelier hangs above it, the gift of the Emperor Frederick Barbarossa. The vault below is now empty, having been opened by the Emperor Otho in 997. He found the body of Charlemagne not reclining in his coffin, as is the usual fashion of the dead, but seated in his throne as one alive, clothed in the imperial robes, bearing the sceptre in his hand, and on his knees a copy of the Gospels.

On his fleshless brow was the crown, the imperial mantle covered his shoulders, the sword Joyeuse was by his side, and the pilgrim's pouch, which he had borne always while living, was still fastened to his girdle. All these venerable relics were removed, and used in the coronation ceremonies of succeeding Emperors of Germany. They are now deposited at Vienna. The throne, in which the body of Charlemagne was seated, alone remains ; it is placed in the gallery running round the octagon, facing the choir. It is an arm-chair, in shape somewhat like that of Edward the Confessor, in Westminster Abbey, but made of slabs of white marble, which, during the coronation, were covered with plates of gold. It is protected by wooden boards, which the sacristan will remove to satisfy a stranger's curiosity. The front of the gallery was originally adorned with 32 pillars of granite and porphyry, brought by Charlemagne from the Exarch's Palace at Ravenna, and partly from the East : these were somewhat wantonly removed by the French, and as only a part of them have been returned from Paris, they have not been replaced. In front of some of the side chapels may be seen small models in coarse wax, of arms, legs, and other parts of the human body, hung up as votive offerings by poor people, who believe that maladies in their limbs have been cured by the interposition of the Saint to whose altars they dedicate these gifts. In the side chapel, dedicated to St. Nicholas, stands an antique sarcophagus of Parian marble, the work of Roman or Greek artists, ornamented with a fine bas-relief of the Rape of Proserpine: the feet of the dead Charlemagne originally rested in it, within his tomb."

And here are some of the Reliques of an ancient order and date, to believe in all which a man must have an iron stomach to digest the tough with the soft.

"The Grandes Reliques are publicly shown to the people only once in 7 years, from the 15th to the 27th of July. So sacred was this ceremony held, and so high was the privilege esteemed of obtaining a glimpse of them, that in former times no fewer than 150,000 pilgrims resorted to the spot from all parts on this occasion; and even so lately as in 1839, the last aniversary, the number of pious visitors exceeded 60,000. These relics were presented to Charlemagne by the Patriarch of Jerusalem, and by Aaron king of Persia. They are deposited in a rich shrine of silver gilt, the work of artists of the 9th century, and consist of—1. The robe worn by the Virgin at the Nativity; it is of cotton, 5 feet long.—2. The swaddling-clothes on which Jesus was wrapped; they are of cloth, as coarse as sacking, of a yellow color.—3. The cloth on which the head of John the Baptist was laid.—4. The scarf worn by our Saviour at the Crucifixion, bearing stains of blood. Intermixed with these religious reliques are many curious antique gems, some Babylonian cylinders, and the like, which serve as jewels to ornament the saintly treasury. The fee for seeing all these wonders amounts to about 10s. English."

Here for the first time the people recognized me as being the Indian from America. They came and stood in groups just by, and watched me as I paced the platform of the station.

As we now leave for Cologne I am so tired and sleepy I shall treat myself with a short rest for my eyes—and awake a few miles from Cologne.

Having arrived. Here is a crowd, and while I was looking after myself, I heard some one naming me by name, and from the crowd of Germans too. On looking up I saw James Buchanan Read of Philadelphia, the Painter Poet. And stretching his long arm he pulled me to him, and soon introduced me to another Poet, Charles

Close, the cotemporary of Mr. Frielegarth, the Poet. I received a message of apologies for his inability of seeing me. But I am at home, for here is a young American, tall and lean as a staff-post. I wandered about with them by moonlight, and gazed with wonder on the curiosities of the place.

This is a noted place.

I will give a short notice of it gathered from the items of my travels.

"Cologne is a fortified town of 65,000 inhabitants, on the left bank of the Rhine, connected by a bridge of boats with the fortress and suburb of Deutz, which has 3700 inhabitants. It is the largest and wealthiest city on the Rhine, and has recently been made a free port.

Cologne owes its existence to a camp pitched here, by the Romans, under Marcus Agrippa, which was afterwards enlarged and rendered permanent by the removal (under Tiberius) of a native tribe, called the Ubii, from the right bank of the Rhine, an event mentioned by Tacitus (Ann. I. 36), and by their settlement on the left bank, at the spot now occupied by Cologne. This first city was called Civitas Ubiorum. More than 80 years after, Agrippina, mother of Nero, and wife of Claudius, who was herself born here, sent hither a colony of Roman veterans, and gave to it her own name, calling it *Colonia* Agrippina. A part only of its ancient appellation is retained in the modern name of Cologne.

In the middle ages, from its wealth, power, and the considerable ecclesiastical foundations of its bishops, it was often called the Rome of the North.

The object which first claims attention here is the Cathedral (Dom Kirche), which, though begun in 1248, during the reign of the Elector and Archbishop of Cologne, Conrad of Hochstedten, has remained up to the present time in a condition between a fragment and a ruin. Had the original plan been completed, (views of the intended edifice are to be procured,) it would have been the St. Peter's of Gothic architecture. Even in its present state, it is one of the finest Gothic monuments in Europe. It is to be regretted that the name of the architect who commenced and planned it, is not with certainty ascertained; as he deserved to be recorded, who conceived so splendid a structure. The two principal towers, according to the original designs, were to have been raised to the height of 500 feet. That which is most finished at present is not above one third of the height. On its top still remains the crane employed by the masons to raise the stones for the building. And it has stood for centuries. It was once taken down, but a tremendous thunder-storm, which occurred soon after, was attributed to its removal by the superstitious citizens, and it was therefore instantly replaced, or a similar one set up in its stead. It is well that it should remain, as it looks as though the present generation had not entirely abandoned the notion of resuming and completing the structure.

The King of Prussia, whose taste for the arts, and zeal for the preservation of ancient edifices, is equal to his liberality, has for many years past expended a considerable sum upon it: this, however, has been employed not in advancing the edifice, but in repairing dilapidations, and preserving what is built, from the ruin into which it threatened to fall owing to previous neglect. The restorations and repairs are conducted in a masterly and most workmanlike manner; the faulty stone of the Drachenfels has been replaced by another of a sounder texture; and the new sculpture and masonry are at least equal to those displayed in the original edifice, while, as mechanical science has made vast strides since the building was founded, it is evident that money alone is wanting to complete it. It is well worth while to ascend the scaffolding, both to view closely the details of the restorations, and to enjoy the view.

The entire length of the body of the church is 400 ft., and its breadth 161.

In a small chapel immediately behind the high altar is the celebrated Shrine of the Three Kings of Cologne, or Magi, who came from the East with presents for the infant Saviour. Their bones were obtained from Milan by the Emperor Frederic Barbarossa, when he took that city by storm, and were presented by him to the then bishop of Cologne, who had accompanied him on his warlike expedition. The case or coffin in which they are deposited is of solid silver gilt, and curiously wrought, surrounded by small arcades, supported on inlaid pillars, and by figures of the Apostles and Prophets. The vast treasures which once decorated it, were sadly diminished at the time of the French revolution, when the shrine and its contents were transported for safety by the Chapter, to Arnsberg, in Westphalia. Many of the jewels were sold to maintain the persons who accompanied it, and have been replaced by paste or glass imitations; but the precious stones, the gems, cameos, and rich enamels which still remain, will give a fair notion of its riches and magnificence in its original state, while those among them of Babylonish origin, visible here as at Aix, afford wide scope for curious inquiry.

The skulls of the three kings, inscribed with their names—*Gaspar*, *Melchior*, and *Balthazer*—written in rubies, are exhibited to view through an opening in the shrine, crowned with diadems (a ghastly contrast), which were of gold, and studded with real jewels, but are now only silver gilt. Among the antiques still remaining are two, of Leda, and Cupid and Psyche, highly beautiful, but singularly inappropriate to their present position.

Those who show the tomb assert that its treasures are still worth six millions of francs= 240,000*l.*; this is an exaggeration, no doubt.

This shrine is opened to the public gaze on Sundays and festivals; but those who desire to see it at other times, or to have a nearer and more minute view of it, must apply to the sacristan, and pay a fee, reduced from 2 thalers to 1 th. 16 S. gr. (= 6 fr.), which admits a party."

Here one might remain a week or more and not get to the end of those curiosities which it does pay a man for viewing. We leave it for the present.

CHAPTER XV.

THE RHINE.

The fatigues of yesterday rest heavily upon my eyelids, and it is with difficulty that I raise them, this morning.

My friend J. B. R. is still a slave of Morpheus, yet his arms are partly free and he shook hands with me.

It is the 21st of August. Daylight was long since about me. The boat on which I am a passenger is a long, narrow affair, with no covering of any account, and is quite full if not more. Just below us is the renowned "Bridge of Boats." An army of boats, side by side, extending from one side of the river to the other, and affording passage for pedestrians, coaches and carts.

Now we are off. Ah, here is a man whom I met in Illinois in '37. The Rev. Mr. Jacobus a German gentleman. I find he does not recognize me, but upon nearer approach he greets me as an old acquaintance.

Having met a gentleman so replete with intelligence, I must not fail to obtain him as an interpreter. He narrates to me his adventures, which interest me very much.

From Cologne for many miles the country is flat, and the scenery very monotonous.

The first considerable town we reach is Bonn, celebrated for its university, library, and being the place where it is said Beethoven lived.

An ancient-looking place it is too. The sketches of history and descriptions given to my readers—that they may judge of it, for themselves.

"Bonn, a town of 12,000 inhabitants, on the left bank of the Rhine, is chiefly remarkable for its University, established by the King of Prussia, in 1818, which has already attained a high reputation on the Continent, owing to the improved discipline maintained among the students, and to the discernment exercised by the government in the appointment of professors. Among those who have already filled chairs here, the most distinguished are Niebuhr (now dead) and Schlegel. The number of students amounts to 720.

The Electors of Cologne formerly resided here, having removed their court hither from Cologne in 1268; their

Palace now serves to contain the University; it is of immense size, with a façade nearly a quarter of a mile long, and includes the Lecture-rooms, Library of about 100,000 volumes, and the Academical Hall, recently decorated with frescos, painted under the direction of Cornelius, a living artist, by his pupils. The subjects are the four faculties, Philosophy, Jurisprudence, Medicine, in which Cuvier and Linnæus are conspicuous, and Theology, where Luther, Calvin, Wickliffe, St. Jerome and the Fathers, and Ignatius Loyola, and other divines, both Catholic and Protestant, are introduced. The artist who painted the Philosophy seems to have shown undue favor to his own countrymen: thus, Homer appears sadly in the background in comparison with Wieland and Herder; Göethe is made prominent, at the expense of Shakspeare and Dante, who hold very subordinate situations and are very indistinctly defined; Virgil and Aristotle are sadly eclipsed by others of the moderns; while Bacon, Socrates, and Cicero, are in a great degree thrown into the shade.

The same building contains the Museum of Rhenish Antiquities, a very large and interesting assemblage of local remains discovered on the banks of the Rhine, and relics of Roman settlements in this part of Germany. They are placed under the care of the veteran Professor Schlegel, to whom application must be made for a ticket of admission. It is much to be lamented that the collection is, as yet, neither named nor catalogued. The following seem to be the most remarkable objects :—A Roman altar, dedicated to Victory, which formerly stood in the square, called Romer Platz, and is supposed by some to be the identical Ara Abiorum mentioned by Tacitus (Annal. I. 39.) A bronze vase, bearing figures of Hercules, Mars, and Venus, in a pure style of art, found at Zulpich. Numerous weapons, trinkets, vases, glass vessels, a winged head of Mercury, found at Hadernheim; the gravestone of one M. Cælius, who fell in the great battle of Varus (bello Variano), against Arminus (? if genuine) ;—Jupiter's wig, and thunderbolt of bronze, from the Hundsruck ; tiles stamped with the numbers of several Roman legions (xxi. xxii.) stationed in these parts ; a Roman mill-stone of Mendig tufa, and an ancient German shield of wood, dug up at Isenburg, in Westphalia, besides 200 bronzes.

An avenue of chestnuts, about half a mile long, forming an agreeable walk, conducts to the Château of Poppelsdorf, which has also been appropriated by the King to the use of the University, and contains the Museum of Natural History. The collection of minerals and fossils is particularly extensive and good, and especially interesting, as illustrating the geology of the Rhine, and of the volcanic deposits of the Siebengebirge and Eifel; arranged by Professor Goldfuss. Among the fossil remains may be seen a complete series from the brown coal formation of Friesdorf, near Bonn. A set of fossil frogs, from the most perfect state down to that of a tadpole, discovered in the shale called paper-coal, deserves notice. Attached to the château is the Botanic Garden —very spacious, very rich, beautifully situated, and admirably kept.

The Minster, surmounted by five towers, is a stately building externally, in the older or round-arched Gothic style; the interior is very plain. It was founded in 320, by Helena, mother of Constantine the Great, and contains a bronze statue of her. The choir, with its two towers, the crypt and the cloisters, date probably from 1151; the rest of the church is later, probably 1270.

Beethoven, the composer, was born in the house No. 934, Rhein Strasse. A monument is erected to his memory in the Market-place. In the church-yard outside the Sternen Thor Niebuhr, the historian is buried. Here also are the graves of several students killed in duels.

The most notable events in the annals of Bonn, are its capture after a long siege, in 1584, by Archbishop Ernest of Bavaria, from Gebhard Truchsess, who had been deposed from the see, because he had become a Protestant; and its surrender to the English and Dutch army under Marlborough, in 1703, after a siege the operations of which were conducted by the celebrated Coehorn. In the course of it a great part of the town was burnt.

At Bonn the beauties of the Rhine may be said to have already commenced."

But, the scenery it is said commences at about 20 miles above Cologne. And now it is in view! Grand and lofty hills or mountains rise from the water's edge. The seven mountains are now around us. And really I am now on the Rhine. A reality, yet like a fairy dream. About this river I have heard and read a great deal. History, romance, and song, dwell along these banks. The towering cliffs frown down the works of man.

These hills bear on their points the ruins of palaces and fortifications. Crumbling they loiter down to the very edge of the water. Towers appear on our right and on our left.

Ages have rolled on the years, and every year has added interest to the events already recorded.

O ! beautiful ! As we turn from one point of view to another, every variety of scenery is presented. Along these deep valleys are fields growing with the grape, and harvest. Every hill looks down. And the sides of the banks seem places as wild as any scenery in America. The hills jutting up from all directions present new features. Town after town, city after city, and village, cluster on the edge of the banks.

Every point of land has with it associations which the traveller beholds with a great deal of interest. Legends, and notions of superstition are creeping into the ideas of people even here. Our guide-books relate to us many a fabulous story connected with miracles of deliverance.

Poetry and song. Over this river each sweet strain has exhausted itself. The Germans rightly think that there is only one Rhine in the world. We give them credit for love of country, and we ask them the same, when we say it would take twenty-five or thirty such rivers to make one Mississippi !

When any nation comes to boasting of rivers, we have one too that could swallow all the German rivers at once.

Along these banks in profusion lay the fragments of ancient glory. The thirty years' war has left its sad memorials along its shore. Armies have stood gazing at each other from bank to bank. These high hills have been clothed with mailed warriors. Furious they have rushed on against one another, and blood has rolled on, and mingled in the stream.

The armies of the Romans have made these shores rumble with their tread; their voice has echoed along its bank.

O thou river of majestic beauty, and grandeur! A tale couldst thou unfold, if but to mortal ears thy silent waters could only speak. Undisturbed kings repose along thy shore, and no voice nor shout shall ever wake them to battle again. Thy waters they have disturbed. Thy glens they have loaded with their gains, and defaced thy natural walls. Lofty and giant trees waved on high their proud and shaggy tops, where now whisper the leaves of the vine. I would be willing to linger on thy shore, could the scene which nations have acted be once more brought in view. From the frozen tops of the Icy Alps, thy waters drip, and gently roll. Along thy course, Princes bow to thee. Till lost in the ocean of immensity.

O ! see, see ! the grand peaks of the hills on the left.—Our boat whirls from eddy to eddy.—The company gaze and admire. The long and narrow steamer cuts the water without much noise.

"Bang," "Bang," echoes the firing of a gun ; and the sound rolls back, and back again, from side to side.

This is done at every steamer that passes here, for the pleasure of travellers, that they might hear the sound.

The hills gradually rise higher and higher. We have just passed the palace where the Queen of England stayed when she was here on a recent visit. Beautiful palaces rest on the sides of the hills. Old ruins, ivy-covered, lay desolate on each hill, and towers leaning to the water's edge. Tales and Legends are told at each crevice of the rocks. Wonders and displays of miraculous power, and a great deal of superstition, much more than the North American Indians ever had.

The Germans adore this river. Its historians, J. V. Müller, Heeren, Rotleck, Ranke, and Winklemann, have left on their shores which other generations will see and admire.

Its poets, the names, Lessing, Gessner, Wieland, Gillert, Vass Stolberg, Göthe, and Schiller, have all left something as a memento of their fond love for this noble river.

I will give here a few specimens of the ardor they feel for this river, by a German writer :—

"There are rivers, whose course is longer, and whose volume of water is greater, but none which unites almost everything that can render an earthly object magnificent and charming, in the same degree as the Rhine. As it flows down from the distant ridges of the Alps, through fertile regions into the open sea, so it comes down from remote antiquity, associated in every age with momentous events in the history of the neighboring nations. A river which presents so many historical recollections of Roman conquests and defeats, of the chivalric exploits in the feudal periods, of the wars and negotiations of modern times, of the coronations of emperors, whose bones repose by its side ; on whose borders stand the two grandest monuments of the noble architecture of the middle ages ; whose banks present every variety of wild and picturesque rocks, thick forests, fertile plains; vineyards, sometimes gently sloping, sometimes perched among lofty crags, where industry has won a domain among the fortresses of nature; whose banks are ornamented with populous cities, flourishing towns and villages, castles and ruins, with which a thousand legends are connected; with beautiful and romantic roads, and salutary mineral springs; a river whose waters offer choice fish, as its banks offer the choicest wines; which, in its course of 900 miles affords 630 miles of uninterrupted navigation, from Bâsle to the sea, and enables the inhabitants of its banks to exchange the rich and various products of its shores; whose cities, famous for commerce, science, and works of strength, which furnish protection to Germany, are also famous as the seats of Roman colonies, and of ecclesiastical councils, and are associated with many of the most important events reeorded in the history of mankind;—such a river it is not surprising that the Germans regard with a kind of reverence, and frequently call in poetry *Father*, or *King Rhine*."

Just before us is the rapid below Castell. The waters roar here in great commotion. The mountains are higher here still, and before night, I set down to read again the description which Byron by the following lines has immortalized this as well as himself, in writing the following description of this beautiful and strange river.

The whole day I have spent in looking over these ruins, and the crags everywhere to be seen.

On the banks of the majestic Rhine,
There Harold gazes on a work divine,
A blending of all beauties; streams and dells,
Fruit, foliage, crag, wood, cornfield, mountain, vine,
And chiefless castles breathing stern farewells
From gray but leafy walls, where Ruin greenly dwells.

And there they stand, as stands a lofty mind,
Worn, but unstooping to the baser crowd,
All tenantless, save to the crannying wind,
Or holding dark communion with the cloud.
There was a day when they were young and proud,
Banners on high, and battles pass'd below;
But they who fought are in a bloody shroud,
And those which waved are shredless dust e'er now,
And the bleak battlements shall bear no future blow.

Beneath these battlements, within those walls,
Power dwelt amidst her passions; in proud state
Each robber chief upheld his armed halls,
Doing his evil will, nor less elate
Than mightier heroes of a longer date.
What want these outlaws conquerors should have?
But History's purchased page to call them great?
A wider space, and ornamented grave?
Their hopes were not less warm, their souls were full as brave.

In their baronial feuds and single fields,
What deeds of prowess unrecorded died!
And Love, which lent a blazon to their shields,
With emblems well devised by amorous pride,
Through all the mail of iron hearts would glide;
But still their flame was fierceness, and drew on
Keen contest and destruction near allied,
And many a tower for some fair mischief won,
Saw the discolor'd Rhine, beneath its ruin run.

But Thou, exulting and abounding river!
Making thy waves a blessing as they flow
Through banks whose beauty would endure forever
Could man but leave thy bright creation so,
Nor its fair promise from the surface mow
With the sharp scythe of conflict,—then to see
Thy valley of sweet waters, were to know
Earth paved like Heaven; and to seem such to me,
Even now what wants thy stream?—that it should Lethe be.

A thousand battles have assail'd thy banks,
But these and half their fame have pass'd away,
And Slaughter heap'd on high his weltering ranks:
Their very graves are gone, and what are they?
Thy tide wash'd down the blood of yesterday,
And all was stainless, and on thy clear stream
Glass'd with its dancing light the sunny ray;
But o'er the blacken'd memory's blighting dream
Thy waves would vainly roll, all sweeping as they seem.

Adieu to thee, fair Rhine! How long delighted
The stranger fain would linger on his way!
Thine is a scene alike where souls united
Or lonely Contemplation thus might stray;

And could the ceaseless vultures cease to prey
On self-condemning bosoms it were here,
Where Nature, nor too sombre, nor too gay,
Wild but not rude, awful yet not austere,
Is to the mellow earth as Autumn to the year

Adieu to thee again! a vain adieu!
There can be no farewell to scene like thine:
The mind is color'd by thy every hue;
And if reluctantly the eyes resign
Their cherish'd gaze upon thee, lovely Rhine!
'Tis with the thankful glance of parting praise;
More mighty spots may rise—more glaring shine,
But none unite in one attaching maze
The brilliant, fair, and soft—the glories of old days.

The negligently grand, the fruitful bloom
Of coming ripeness, the white city's sheen,
The rolling stream, the precipice's gloom,
The forest's growth, and Gothic walls between,
The wild rocks shaped as they had turrets been
In mockery of man's art; and these withal
A race of faces happy as the scene,
Whose fertile bounties here extend to all,
Still springing o'er thy banks, though Empires near them fall.

BYRON.

O what power and beauty is there in those lines after one has looked on this majestic river!

The night intercepts our view. The towns and villages of the Germans show their lights and fires, and the city of Mayence is in sight, on our right; on our left is the fortified town of Castell, where we land and reluctantly leave our boat, and 20 miles more then we shall be in the free city of Frankfort.

After a delay of two hours we have at last started, and an hour's journey or more we are in Frankfort! and only 4,300 miles from home. But thank heaven I am safe.

CHAPTER XVI.

PEACE CONGRESS.

THE proceedings of the Third General Peace Congress, were opened on Thursday, the 22d of August, 1850, at Frankfort-on-the-Maine, in St. Paul's Church, the building made memorable by the recent meetings of the Frankfort Parliament. It is a handsome circular building, with a gallery supported by marble columns, and was fitted up in its present state for the German Parliament. Behind the President's chair, was a large shield emblazoned with the German eagle, whilst above the crimson drapery on which this heraldic decoration rested, were three flags, each black, crimson and gold. The staves surrounded by triumphal wreaths. The aspect of the interior of St. Paul's Church on the 22d, attracted, however, much less attention than did one of its visitors, when it was whispered round the place that General Haynau was present.

He sat for some time near one of the side doors, listening, apparently with much attention, but left before the termination of the proceedings. The seats lately occupied by the members of the Frankfort Parliament, were on the present occasion filled by a numerous company, made up of Germans, Englishmen, Americans, Frenchmen, and Belgians. The seat put up for the Archduke John, and subsequently occupied by M. Gagern, was now filled by the President (for that year) of the Peace Congress, Herr Jaup, late Minister of Hesse-Darmstadt. There were about 500 English present, out of an audience of 2000.

Among the delegates to the meeting, were R. Cobden, Esq., M. P.; Chas. Hindley, Esq., M. P.; Lawrence Heyworth, Esq., M. P.; Dr. Lee, F. R. S.; Revs. J. Burrett, E. Miall, and H. Richards; Elihu Burritt, Joseph Sturge, J. Wilson, Dr. Dick, and others, from England. The list of American deputies included,—Massachusetts, Rev. Mark Trafton, Boston, Rev. Dr. Hitchcock, Rev. Mr. Sargent, John Tappan, Esq.; Maine, Rev. David Thurston; Rhode Island, Rev. Dr. Hall; New Hampshire, Hon. John Prentiss; Connecticut, Rev. G. W. Pennington; New York, G. Williams, Henry Garret;

Pennsylvania, Prof. C. D. Cleveland, Samuel Sartain; Kentucky, W. H. G. Butler, Patrick Joyes; Missouri, Rev. Dr. Bullard, and from the North American Indians, the Chief Kah-ge-ga-gah-bowh, or Geo. Copway, in costume. From Illinois, T. Eastman; Indiana, A. R. Forsyth; Michigan, N. H. B. Dowling; American Peace Society, L. S. Jacobs.

From France the following gentlemen attended: M. M. Cormenin, *ancien deputé*, member of the French Council of State; Emile de Girardin, Editor of *La Presse;* Joseph Garnier, Professor of Political Economy; Guilaumin, Editor of the *Economist;* Coqueril, fils; Lacan, Ernest, Pontonie, fils. From Brussels, M. Visschers, M. Depetiaux, Inspector-General of Prisons in Belgium. Germany contributed delegates from Darmstadt, Leipsic, Wiesbaden, Mainx, Homberg, Bonn, Giessen, Frankfort, and other places.

The Congress sat three days, there being a morning and evening session each day.

The correspondence of the London Times, spoke of us —the following:

"A North American Indian, who entered with the other delegates, but who has not yet spoken, was received with plaudits almost equal to those which hailed the entrance of Cobden."

FIRST DAY.

The centre of St. Paul's Church was appropriated to the members of the foreign delegation, and to the German members of the Congress; the galleries both on the ground floor and above, being accommodated to the accommodation of visitors, among whom was a large number of ladies.

The business of the Congress commenced each day at ten o'clock, A. M. The first resolution submitted to the Congress, was to the following effect :—

"The Congress of the friends of Universal Peace, assembled at Frankfort-on-the-Main, on the 22d, 23d, and 24th of August, 1850, acknowledge that recourse to arms being condemned alike by religion, morality, reason, and humanity, it is the duty of all men to adopt measures calculated to abolish war; and the Congress recommends all its members to labor in their respective Countries by means of a better education of youth, by the pulpit, the platform, and the press, as well as by other practical methods to eradicate those hereditary hatreds, and political and commercial prejudices which have been so generally the cause of disastrous wars."

The following members spoke in favor of this resolution, which was carried by a unanimous vote. The Rev. John Burrett, Le Pasttor, Bonnet of Paris, M. de Carmenin, of Paris; H. J. Garret, of New York, (whose appearance, he being of a pure negro blood, excited considarable sensation and interest.)

The second resolution, as follows, was presented in a speech of great power by M. Visschers, of Brussels.

"This Congress is of opinion that one of the most effectual means of preserving peace, would be for Governments to refer to arbitration all those differences between them which cannot otherwise be amicably settled."

This was supported by M. Bach, of Darmstadt; M. Mourch, of Frankfort; M. Emile de Girardin (this gentleman rising to reply to some difficulties which had been suggested in the practical application of arbitration); Prof. Cleveland, of the United States; and Richard Cobden, M. P.

Mr. Cobden said it was not his intention to have spoken that day, but he must say a word or two on the supposed difficulties of arbitration. No doubt there were difficulties—but were there not difficulties in war too? and what he wished to put before the diplomatists of Europe and America was, which of these difficulties will you choose—war or arbitration? One of them it must be; for you confess that neither your diplomacy, nor your mediation enable you to settle your quarrels—generally about some point of etiquette or trumpery debt of a few thousand pounds. What he wanted was, if the people of England or America saw their Governments again involved in a quarrel with some weaker power, whether on the shores of Portugal or Greece, and refusing the offer made by such a power to settle the dispute by arbitration, but resorting to the sword to enforce their demands, then he did hope that the people would drive such governments from power, and supply their places with men who would do the business in a more workmanlike manner. Mr. Cobden alluded to the progress which the Peace cause had made during the past year, and said that two remarkable illustrations of this progress had occurred in the last peace meeting which he attended in London, and in the meeting which he was then addressing at Frankfort. At the meeting in London he sat side by side with General Klapka, the general who had unsuccessfully fought the battles in Hungary. At the meeting of this present Congress, at Frankfort, no less a person than General Haynau had for some time occupied a place among the visitors (General H. had left the hall before Mr. Cobden rose to speak). He (Mr. C.) thought it very significant, when they found at their meetings such men as the military leaders, both of liberty and despotism. It incited in these men's minds something like the dawn of a suspicion that their own profession was not of the most stable and satisfactory character. (Cheers).

THE SECOND DAY.

Charles Hindley, Esq. proposed the second resolution: "That the standing armaments with which the governments of Europe menace one another impose intolerable burdens and inflict grievous moral and social evils upon their respective communities; this Congress cannot therefore too earnestly call the attention of governments to the necessity of entering upon a system of international disarmament, without prejudice to such measures as may be considered necessary for the maintenance of the security of the citizens and the internal tranquillity of each State."

The Hon. gentleman brought forward a vast body of statistics, with a view to show that war had always contributed to national ruin, for which reason it was necessary to abolish the existing standing armies, the prime cause of war. He expressed the belief that the time would arrive at which national hatred would cease and all men be brethren.

Mr. Hindley was loudly applauded.

The Rabbi Stein, of Frankfort, said that war ought not to be admitted, even in self-defence, as the limit at which self-defence began would be difficult to define.

Instead, he remarked, of making weapons of war, let men be employed in cultivating land, and if Europe were not large enough, there was America. Let the governments of Europe, instead of dividing men by the sword, employ them in making railways.

M. Joseph Garnier showed that permanent armies render unproductive a great part of the force of man, and that consequently armies diminish the welfare of societies. He showed also that the governments, by standing armies, are obliged to crush the people by taxation.

The *Rev. Mr. Buller* of the State of Missouri, dwelt

on the fact that the United States has no permanent army, though they were larger than any European State.

M. Emile de Girardin, next spoke. He remarked that the immense sums which armies had cost would have enabled great works of peace to be accomplished, and all social problems to be solved. After the revolution of February, he had, he said, cried "Disarm, disarm! Have confidence in the justice of our cause, and in the sentiments of all the nations of Europe." But he had not been listened to, and had been accused of treason. Well, two armies had been sent to the Rhine and the Alps, and what glory had Frenchmen gained? They had given themselves two enemies—misery and hunger, and had lighted up war in their streets.

Mr. Cobden said that standing armies were more dangerous in peace than in war. War was a state of madness and passion for which some excuse might be made, but a standing armament was a permanent injustice.

The third resolution was then adopted.

The fourth resolution was then brought forward. It was as follows—

"This Congress reiterates its strong disapprobation of

all foreign loans negotiated for the purpose of furnishing to one people the means of slaughtering another."

M. Drucker of Amsterdam, considered that the participation among the different nations of twenty-five millions of paper money was a powerful guarantee for peace.

M. E. de Girardin said that certain democrats regarded war as the only means of reconquering their lost liberties, but the money he thought might be employed in more useful purposes. War could not be carried on without means, and therefore if loans of money were refused it could not take place; he should therefore support the resolution.

M. Z. de Stettin remarked that a general customs union between all nations of the world would be the best guarantee against war.

The fourth resolution was carried, and second day's sittings brought to a close.

THIRD, AND LAST DAY.

Notwithstanding the inclemency of the weather, the meeting of the Congress was well attended. Some excitement was produced by the appearance of the Rev.

Mr. Copway, formerly a native American Indian Chief, who spoke at great length and with much energy on the immorality and irreligion of war. The preceding speakers had been limited in their observations to speeches of twenty minutes each; but, in consequence of the peculiar circumstances of this case, he was allowed to address the meeting for forty minutes. The speech of this person was received with much enthusiasm. He proposed the fifth resolution, namely—

"This Congress acknowledging the principle of non-intervention, recognizes it to be the sole right of every state to regulate its own affairs."

Mr. Copway was followed by two German gentlemen, Dr. Nell and Dr. Bodensee. The latter speaker urged the Congress to undertake the settlement of the Schleswig-Holstein question. The proposition did not apparently meet with a very cordial reception.

The Chairman suggested that the introduction of that question would involve a breach of their rules which prohibited the discussion of any existing political question.

Mr. Cobden also observed, that it would be impossible for the Congress then to go on with the subject, as neither party appeared to be duly represented at the meeting.

The resolution was adopted.

The sixth resolution was as follows: "This Congress recommends all the friends of Peace to prepare public opinion in their respective countries for the convocation of a Congress of the representatives of the various states, with a view to the formation of a code of international law."

Mr. E. Miall, repudiated the notion that there was anything visionary or Utopian in the peace movement, and made a strong protest against what are called "practical men."

Elihu Burritt, entered into a history of the peace theory, which he maintained owed its origin to France and Germany and not to America.

Mr. Chapin of New York, astonished the assembly by a burst of Yankee eloquence, and the novel coloring which he gave to rather old materials.

The resolution was carried, together with an additional one against duelling. On the latter *M. Carmenin* and *M. Girardin* spoke. A vote of thanks to the municipal authorities of Frankfort followed, in honor of whom Mr. Cobden led an English "Hip, hip, hurrah," to the intense astonishment of the Germans.

It was then resolved that the proceedings should be printed and circulated at a small charge; and a vote of thanks to Dr. Jaup having been passed, the proceedings were declared at an end.

The Congress it was announced would be held in London next year, which will take place about the month of August, 1851.

CHAPTER XVII.

AFTER SKETCHES OF SPEECHES AND MEN.

THE last of the Congress is about over, and I have made my poorest speech. For never in my life did I speak to such disadvantage. The people had already heard Girardin, the French orator, Cobden, and a host of others. The speeches of these men had given a commonplace character to the speeches which were to come after them. The people had become tired of listening, and seemed to have no desire for anything new. Besides this, no new feature could be brought forward in support of the great cause of Peace, and all the arguments had been worn threadbare. The good speeches had preceded me, and the very best, which was to be delivered by the Rev. E. H. Chapin, of New York city, was just at my heels. In this predicament I could not look upon myself with any great degree of confidence, nor as being in a very enviable situation.

The fifth resolution, which was moved by me, was as follows :—

"This Congress acknowledging the principle of non-intervention, recognizes it to be the sole right of every State to regulate its own affairs."

I will not trouble the reader with even an outline of the remarks with which I endeavored to enforce the resolution. It is enough to say that they were listened to with more attention than I expected, and more than they deserved. It is doubtful whether any but members of a Peace Congress would be so lenient.

I will give a short passage from the papers which kindly noticed me, not in the way of boasting, but to record the good-will and kind feeling of the people with whom I sojourned :

"The personal appearance and manner of the different members of the Congress, gave occasion to many interesting sketches. None seemed to attract more notice than an Indian Chief, who it appears was one of the delegates from America. His Indian name is given as Ka-ge-ga-ga-bowh, and some accounts call him a chief of the Ottoways, while others mention him as being of the Ojibbeways. In some papers he is also called

Rev. Copway. One correspondent speaks of him as follows:

"The ladies direct their looks no longer to the finely bearded men on the left; the beardless Indian Chief, with the noble Roman profile, and the long, shining, black hair, takes their attention. He bears in his hand a long, and mystically ornamented staff, which looks like a princely sceptre, and wears a dark blue frock, with a scarf over his shoulders, and bright metallic plates upon his right arm. The Frankforters are sorry that he wears a modern hat, instead of a cap with feathers, yet this mixture of European elegance with Indian nature has a striking effect, which is increased by the reflection that he has come from the forests of the New World, with a message of peace to the Old, though he finds more gaping curiosity than sympathy."

His manner on entering the tribune is described as follows:

"An aristocratic bearing—and is not the orator a Prince?—an earnest, calm countenance, well-toned voice, few, but natural gestures, and an epic manner, as if he stood in the midst of his tribe, relating clearly, and without passion, some important occurrence. But by degrees he becomes warmer, steps back and forth in the tribune, raises his voice, which he now accompanies with more passionate gestures, and finally with words that I did not understand, brings forward his Indian pipe of peace, and amid the greatest enthusiasm presents it to the President of the assembly."

In the course of two hours after, my speech was in the language of the Germans. I might have done something towards leaving a good impression of the speaking powers of an aboriginal American, had not a portly Yankee come forward and taken from my hand the laurels. But glad I am that it is an American who has won the best expression of feeling and approbation of the people.

The speeches of Girardin and the matter-of-fact Cobden had shaken the pillars of the immense building in which the multitude were assembled; but *the speech* was yet to be delivered.

The name " E. H. Chapin" was called, and the person who answered to that name passed by my side and went up to the tribune. No sooner had he commenced speaking than there was felt to be something beyond the power of language, or the mere expression of ideas. The audience listened. Now and then an applause escaped the assembly. He enumerated the reasons why we should expect peace, and the blessings which would flow from it. In a few words, in vivid flashes, he pictured the whole course of improvement and reform which had followed the invention of the printing press. The Bible was on its way—the sails of every land, and the mighty power of steam, were urging on the period of universal peace—oceans, lakes, rivers, air, electricity, all things were in motion to spread the event which is the desire of all nations. The steamer was dragging its rope of gold across the sea, from one continent and island to another—and as he closed, the applause of the assembly made the very building tremble.

In the midst of this thundering applause he again passed me, and as soon as he sat down I arose, not knowing what I was doing, and said, "It was well worth while to come 4,000 miles to deliver such an address," and then sitting down and turning to my English friends I whispered, "There! try and beat that if you can!"

Certainly this was very injudicious, inasmuch as it might have been construed into an insult, but I could not help it, for my nerves had been so run away with that I lost all my self-command.

The following sketch of the Rev. Mr. Chapin, in an English paper, will be recognized by those who have seen and heard him. It is very life-like :

"Edwin H. Chapin is one of the ablest and most eloquent expounders and defenders of the doctrine of unlimited salvation. He has no faith in the old black fellow who keeps the fire-office down stairs. He imagines that poets and divines give him more credit for sagacity and potency than he deserves, and that if he ever was a genius he is now in his dotage, and furthermore that he has not goodness enough to be entitled to our respect, nor influence sufficient over our future destiny to alarm our fears. To him a devil by any other name is just as dreadful, and the Satan he endeavors to subdue he calls Evil, Sin, Crime, Vice, Error. He thinks the distillery, where the worm dieth not and the fires are unquenched, is a hell on earth which causes weeping, wailing and gnashing of teeth.

Mr. Chapin is an independent, straight-forward man, who has a will and a way of his own, and he is willing to allow others the same freedom he assumes himself. He doos not expect his church to cough when he takes cold, nor to perspire when he is warm, nor to sneeze

REV DR. CHAPIN

when he takes snuff, nor to acquiesce in silent submission to every proposition that he makes. He is not a theological tyrant, threatening vengeance and outer-darkness and eternal fire to all the members of his flock who will not uncomplainingly and unhesitatingly yield to his spiritual supervisorship. His lessons and lectures may sometimes smell of the lamp, but they never smell of brimstone. His education, his temperament, his organization of brain, his natural benevolence, and the society in which he has lived, moved, and had his being, have contributed to make him a preacher of the gospel. He advocates with heroic courage and untiring zeal the doctrines of his faith, but is universally respected by all denominations of professing Christians.

Mr. Chapin is happily constituted. The animal and the angel of his nature are so nicely balanced, and his poetical temperament is so admirably controlled by his practical knowledge, that his intellectual efforts are invariably stamped with the mint-mark of true currency. There is a harmonious blending of the poetical and the practical, a pleasant union of the material with the spiritual, an arm-in-arm connection of the ornamental and the useful, a body and soul joined together, in his discourses. He avoids two extremes, and is not so material as to be cloddish or of the earth earthy, nor so aërial as to be vapory or of the clouds cloudy. There is something tangible, solid, nutritious and enduring in his sermons. He is not profound in the learning of the schools. Many of his inferiors could master him on doctrinal questions. The outbursting and overwhelming effusions of his natural eloquence, the striking originality of his conceptions, the irresistible power of his captivating voice, the vivid and copious display of illustration, thrill and charm the appreciative hearer. He presents his arguments and appeals with an articulation as distinct and understandable as his gesticulation is awkward. He is sometimes abrupt, rapid and vehement, but never "tears a passion to tatters." His tenacious memory enables him to quote with great promptitude, and he has that delicate, sensitive taste which enables him to select with unerring precision whatever is truly sublime and beautiful in an author.

Mr. Chapin declaims splendidly in spite of his hands, which are always in his way. The stiff and technical restraints of style which disfigure the pulpit efforts of some divines never appear in his sermons, but seem rather to pinion his elbows and cramp his fingers. He has a fervid imagination, great facility of expression, is scrupulously correct in his pronunciation. He never indulges in hypocritical cant. There is no theatrical uplifting of the hands and uprolling of the eyes. He seems to have a thorough knowledge of his subject, and commands your admiration by the kingly majesty and sublime beauty of his thought. Now he flings a page of meaning into a single aphorism,—now he electrifies his spell-bound hearers with a spontaneous burst of eloquence,—now he dissolves their eyes to tears by a wizard stroke of pathos,—now he controls their hearts with the sovereign power of a monarch who rules the mind-realm. He infuses his soul into his voice, and both into the nerves and heart of the hearers.

In person, he is stout, fleshy and well-proportioned. His countenance is mild, benignant and thoughtful, with an expression of integrity, denoting his inability to perform a mean action. He is near-sighted, and his defect is no small disadvantage to him when he reads, and may account for his ungrateful action in the pulpit, since it compels him to face his manuscript so closely he almost eats his own words and salutes his own rich figures and glowing sentiments, and fulfils literally the scriptural maxim, "He shall kiss his own lips who giveth a correct answer." But, as I have just intimated, he usually reads his discourses, although he is an easy extemporaneous speaker; but he is apt to become so intensely excited he rarely trusts to his impulses. He commands a very ready pen, and is the author of two or three small volumes which are widely circulated. He has a full, florid face, which indicates good health and happy contentment. His hair is dark brown. He wears glasses, so I cannot tell the color of his eyes. He has a broad, high forehead, indicating the intellectual strength of its owner. He is about forty-five years of age, and has labored with honor and success for many years in Richmond, Va., Charlestown, Mass., as well as Boston, but is now preaching in the city of New York, where he is very popular and useful."

The speeches of Emile de Girardin and Cobden on the first day are thus spoken of in the correspondence of the London Times, and for their style of speaking it is a very good description:—

"The appearance in the tribune of M. Emile Girardin was the signal for loud acclamations on the part of the French auditors. He was the representative of France *par excellence*, and his *distingué* appearance contrasted strangely with the primitive look of many of his fellow orators. His speech was equally different from those of his predecessors. Biblical allusions were not in his way, but he came in as a propounder of philosophical abstractions, which he pointed off with French epigrammatic neatness. The idea of *unité* was to be carried out—*unité* in everything; and every time he said the word *unité* it was with remarkable gusto. Then he got into universal history, and, declaring that certain conquerors of the Old World were named Alexander, Cæsar, and Napoleon, added that the victors of the New World were named Watt, Wilberforce, &c. Civilization was the great gain of modern Europe, and type and steam are now to do what was done heretofore by fire and sword. All this, delivered with an uniform style of gesticulation peculiarly his own, told with great force; and he could retire with all the satisfaction of a brilliant Frenchman who had exhibited *son talent*.

But, after all, the great card of the performance was the speech of Mr. Cobden, which came in towards the conclusion. Indeed, had it not been for this speech, I fear the day's sport would have wound up rather coldly. The president, after the passing of the first resolution, which occurred about 1 o'clock, allowed the parties assembled to retire for 10 minutes, and many thus retiring never came back again. Hence considerably more empty seats were visible in the afternoon than in the morning, and two or three orations which opened the second act, and included another speech by Girardin, a very long history of William Penn, digested into an address from the Pennsylvania Peace Society, were by no means of such a nature as to diffuse animation. But Cobden's speech set all right. It was a bold, slashing address, not marked throughout by good taste, but abounding in arguments and illustrations which everybody could understand. In calling attention to the second resolution, he said, that he did not wish to interfere with the work of the diplomatists, but merely insisted on the adoption of an international umpire when other peaceful means should fail, protesting against war as a nuisance which every people had a right to stop in defiance of the existing governments. If no better peaceable plan could be found the Governments were bound to adopt that proposed by the Peace Congress; and if any Government refused to adopt a plan of arbitration the people should repudiate that

Government. This was pretty strong language, and the vehemence of tone and gesture with which it was uttered stood out in strong relief against the sharp epigrammatic manner and jerking action of M. Emile Girardin. A symbol had been furnished to Mr. Cobden on his journey up the Rhine, and the comparison of the union of the Rhine and the Moselle with that of all mankind in universal brotherhood was pleasing to the audience when they rested from uproariously applauding more peppery displays. An allusion to the presence at the meeting of General Haynau, as an evidence that even the warriors themselves had become averse from their profession—though this was in the worst possible taste—brought the whole oration to a showy conclusion. The second resolution was carried immediately afterwards, and the meeting was adjourned till to-morrow, the audience being kindly reminded of the dinner, which has been prepared for them at the Main-lust."

CHAPTER XVIII.

SKETCHES—CONTINUED.

THE town, or rather, as the Frankforters themselves never fail to call it, the Free Town of Frankfort, was unusually gay. Animated and crowded with lounging travellers the streets always are; but now there seemed an unusual number, and generally not walking singly, but in small groups, as if some bond of union held them together, and as though one and the same aim had brought them to the same spot. And then, too, one saw a great number of——they were like Englishmen, and yet there was a difference. These were Americans; and among them, as well as those whose country in Cæsar's time was not considered quite worthless, since it produced an oyster, were not a few whose trim dress and staid sobriety of demeanor marked at once the respectable sect to which they belonged. And look at yonder dark figure with countenance so calm and imperturbable! Whence cometh he? In his hand he holds a long instrument, which some may deem a weapon; and round his left arm is a band, seemingly a badge of authority. How black and long the hair that falls without a wave down upon his shoulders! He is from the far, far West. Perhaps his home has been where the Rocky Mountains fling their huge shadow as the sun disappears behind them, while their peaks flame like meteors in the sky. What leads *him* hither?—why leaves he his hunting-grounds to come to this European city?—from the plain that quakes beneath the quick tramp of the buffalo to where the gentle footfall of the pleasure-seeker is mingled with the measured tread of well-disciplined European soldiery?

What a glorious day! How bright the sky—and the atmosphere how clear and transparent! Even the fine taper points of the lightning conductors, with which every house is furnished, are distinctly visible from afar. How that golden cross shines above the house-tops, looking more like a sign from heaven than a thing of bronze placed there by a mechanic's hands! The edifice over which it rises was once a church, but is so no longer. Let us enter there. It is already well filled with people; in the body of the building are men only, among whom we seem to recognize some we met yesterday in little groups about the streets ; while around the edifice beneath the gallery, supported by the massive columns, ladies have taken their places. Before us is a raised tribune, over which are hanging three flags, each with three stripes, black, red, and gold. Still higher is a female figure, with golden hair, like a true daughter of the north ; a sword too, is in her hand, but it rests in repose. And on each side, within a wreath of laurel, is a German rhyme, to the effect that, even as this green garland is interwoven, so may all the people of Germany be entwined in bonds of amity. For you must know that here, beneath this very roof, not long ago did sit the deputies from city, and town, and university—from borough and village, from every part of Germany. Here, elate with hope, and promising themselves great things, with fond expectations of the realizing of long-cherished wishes, good, and wise, and well-intentioned men met together to talk of plans for their country's weal. But though calm hearts were here, there were men, too, whose thoughts were of violence ; and but few, if any, possessed that plain, practical ability which, when something is to be done, is of more avail than great stores of learning. And so nothing was done. But the space within these walls, where till then words of prayer, and exhortation, and praise had been heard, became an arena for fierce contention; and maddening words that led to blood resounded there amid the hoarse roar of popular applause. You have read of the wild scenes of revolutionary France, and how orators were cheered on by their party, till, with swimming brain and in a frenzy of excitement, they uttered fearful threats and terrible denunciations; and how the calm and resolute were hooted, and their words drowned in the mad screams and execrations of a rabble audience. And so it was here—beneath this very dome over which the bright cross we saw just now was gleaming. How different is the present assembly! For what are they waiting?

The bell has been rung, and silence instantly obtained. We are now told the meaning of this assembling of men from many lands. They come here to propose peace to the nations—to propose that war shall henceforth be no more. It is a Peace Congress at which we are present; and on this errand these men have been brought together from the remote parts of the earth. We will not argue on the practicability of thus establishing universal peace:

so strange are the revolutions which time brings about, that even this too may happen. But there was something that interested us more at this meeting than the dim and uncertain result—far off at all events, even if ever attainable—and it was this: to observe the difference in the mode of thought and manner of utterance of the speakers, assembled from different countries, with one object and in one cause. Meetings are too common now-a-days to offer much of novelty; but we seldom see one like this, where many men in their own peculiar language give utterance to their peculiar thoughts. And it is for this reason—and this reason only—that we have brought you hither.

The first speaker is a Scotsman—so at least we should judge by his accent. Why, that one man's face is worth all the speeches we may hear to-day, so indicative is it of kindly feeling, light-heartedness, and hearty good-fellowship. How sunny the smile on his face as he utters his conviction that men were not made to fight, seeing that their fingers are not adapted for tearing, nor their teeth for fastening on each other! There is good-humor in his argument, and good-feeling too; and if his reasoning be not incontrovertible in the cause of universal peace, we still like war the less if it be only because it is repugnant to him with whom, on any point whatever, we should be sorry to be at variance. His language is plain and unstudied, and his meaning clear as the bright eye that animates his rosy countenance. No German could ever speak so ; neither is there method enough in the arrangement to please the German mind. How could he touch on such a topic without abstract principles and philo sophic rules ? But let us listen to the German, and then compare the two.

With thoughtful mien, with slow and rather heavy step, he approaches the tribune. There is none of the ease that was so prepossessing in the first speaker, for the German would as soon think of putting aside his gravity as of putting off his coat in public. Besides, he has to speak before an assembly ; and the professor is perhaps thinking of the Forum, and of the dignity of the toga, and of the pride of ancient Rome. He looks very grave, for he doubtless has well weighed the difficulties to be encountered ; and instead of jumping to the conclusion, has wrestled with the obstacles one by one, and forced his way through by dint of argument. The toil is over, but it is still present to his mind. This man is not one to make proselytes or gain adherents; for both would be deterred by a sense of the difficulties to be encountered, and by the fear that they might not prove so manful in the attack as he. You feel at once—though, mind you, he has hardly spoken yet—that it is a serious affair you are about, and that if you follow in his steps you will have enough to do. He is not one to make light of a difficult matter, and trusting somewhat to fortune, call gaily for you to come on. He tells you beforehand it is difficult; but then he will also tell you how difficulties may be subdued, and indeed *must* be so if his calculations be correct.

But now he is speaking, or rather he is reading his speech. Do you understand his meaning? Not always, I think; for it is the deduction of abstruse reasoning, and one would need to read the same twice over to comprehend it well. Besides, the sentences are long and intricate; there is an entanglement which you cannot well unravel; and many a relative pronoun, too, which puzzles you, as you are not quite certain to which member of the sentence it relates. It is too involved to be clear. But perchance the speaker's thoughts are not quite definite either: hence that vagueness which leaves you at the end where you were when he began. He does not point out the road you are to travel for the accomplishment of your purpose, but he gives you theories which are to be your guide. You do not advance; you are not carried forwards either with or against your will; but keeping the one point in view, instead of approaching *towards* it, you move *round* it always at the same distance. Alas! alas! it was this very fault which before, in these same walls, led to nothing. Here, in the Peace Congress of the Nations, I understood how Germany, like the virgins who slept, entered not to the feast when at last the bridegroom came for whose arrival they had so long been watching.

If you are tired of listening to the speaker, then look at that man sitting on the right of the president, and leaning back in his chair quite at his ease; his right elbow on the table, and his head resting on his hand. His thin dark hair is combed over his forehead on the right, his eyebrows are drawn somewhat together, and he seems not to be merely looking at, but scrutinizing, those before him. His mouth is *firmly* closed, by which I mean that the lips do not merely gently touch each other, but that they do so with a pressure. Such a mouth is always indicative of steady resolve. As he sits there, moving only his eyes, but not turning his head, there is, methinks, a rather dark expression about the brow. Perhaps I may be wrong ; yet strangely enough, that countenance recalls one I have elsewhere seen, over which, and with good reason, an expression of gloom was spread. Now look yourself, and tell me is there not in that head a strange resemblance to one well known to you ? Does it not remind you of Napoleon ? For my part I thought at once of that picture where he is sitting after a defeat with knitted brow and eyes gazing fixedly before him. It is said that he whom you are looking at, and who at this distance looks so like the Emperor, is related to him ; and I dare say he is not disinclined to assist the resemblance as much as is in his power.

The president reads the name of Emile Girardin as being next on the list of those who have announced their intention to speak ; and he whom we have been observing rises and mounts the tribune. He moves with a quick step ; he makes haste to obey the summons. He seems quite at home in his present place, as if he were accustomed to be often where he is. There is nothing like hesitation in his manner, although he does pause for a moment or two, and looks around him before he begins to speak. Why he does so I do not know; perhaps it is only his usual manner; perhaps, however, it may be done for effect. He holds in his hand a small piece of paper, on which some notes are written; but once having begun to speak, he is in no want of ideas: thoughts, and words to express them, come crowding on; and the short-hand writers yonder will have enough to do to follow him. His utterance is rapid; and now and then having said something terse and to the point, he comes to a dead stop. He has pronounced words that strike you, and he knows they do so; he knew they would before he uttered them, and he is giving you time to let you feel their effect, and, if you like, to applaud. His countenance does not grow animated by speaking; his brow is knit the same as before; and there is still something dark about the eyes, and the upper part of the face as he looks straight before him. Action, that difficult part of the orator's art, he has yet to learn. He moves his right hand up and down at regular intervals, and then again it takes hold of the tribune in company with the left. There is something very commonplace in this monotony of action, corresponding as it does in no way whatever with the matter of his discourse. But how well-turned are his phrases, how elegant his diction! It is true he often says something that would not mean much if translated into English; although as *he* puts it in the elegant language of France, it *does* arrest your attention. His sentences are mostly short; and it is in these short ones that there is most point. He utters them abruptly, and at the same time with much decision; as if those words were to settle the question at once. 'La science détruit la politique,' he will tell you; or, 'Il y a une nouvelle politique dans le monde—c'est la science.' This is not said as a theory, but uttered as a law. It is pronounced like a commandment, and as such you are to receive it. To the applause which greets him he seems accustomed, and waits quietly each time till the noise has subsided before he again begins to speak. He intends that each word shall be heard, and till all is quiet that cannot be. A phrase of usual length, followed by one of but five or six words, spoken quickly, but with the firmest intonation, and the discourse is at an end. He quits the tribune as quickly as he entered it, and taking his seat, is again an imperturbable spectator as before.

What a thunder of applause now resounds through the building as yonder speaker is about to ascend the tribune!

That is Cobden. There is nothing in his person that could lead you to believe he would battle still when resolution appeared to be in vain; nothing that might incline you to notice him in a crowd of men. But let him speak, and you at once acknowledge the man to be 'a power'—a power that dictates, and must be treated with like a neighboring state. He is below the middle height, and of spare habit; one of those men, in short, who Sallust tells us are to be feared in a state. Every syllable he utters is as distinct as the organs of speech can make it. He speaks rather slowly at first, and at times somewhat hesitatingly; but this is not because he does not know what to say, but because he is thinking how he shall express his meaning with the very utmost amount of power. He does not seek fine words, but strong ones. And strength there is in what he says, and in his manner of saying it. His sentences are short, like the Roman sword; but they are forged for close warfare and a hard struggle. He leans forward as he speaks; and with his right arm, as he dashes it downwards, seems to beat his arguments into his hearers' minds. Right or wrong, his whole heart is in the cause. Of that there can be no doubt. He speaks from conviction; and with an earnestness and intensity such as one rarely hears. There is nothing elegant in his language; it is clothed with no ornament, but, like the naked limbs of the gladiator, it trusts entirely to its unaided strength. All he proposes is intelligible; all his reasoning is plain and clear. He knows nothing of theory, but deals solely with facts. He hurls into the arena before you—at your very feet, as it were—some fact, some massive fact; and he tells you to get rid of it—to move it thence if you can. That is his mode of arguing. There is such energy in his manner, such life and energy in his words, that you now understand the power of the Corn-Law League.

Such speaking is new here. It takes every one by surprise; but after a while you hear from time to time exclamations in various languages, all expressive of wonderment at the boldness of his thoughts, and the manner in which they are imparted to you. But he cares only for convincing his audience, and cares not for its applause. He is full of his plan, and does not like delay; hence he is impatient of the 'bravos' and the shouts; and he can hardly wait till the storm of approbation has subsided. But as he retires to his place, it does not die away so soon, and all give expression to their feelings in one long round of applause.

As in the plays of the French dramatists there is more attention to the rules of art than in our own, so is it in the speeches we have heard to-day. In style and in ar-rangement the French were certainly the best: they were the most finished of all. Victor Hugo was to have been there, and it would have been interesting to hear the author of 'à la Colonne' speak on the benefits of universal peace. But as he stated in his letter, 'his physicians had *condemned* him to repose'—an expression, by the by, which it would never have entered the head of an Englishman or a German to make use of. Cobden's words fell from his lips with all the force of a sledge-hammer. There was truly nothing in his oratory, but all he said had weight and substance, or rather had weight *because* it was composed of real tangible stuff.

The Peace Congress afforded much matter for thought, independently of the especial object for which it was held: one could here study to advantage the distinctive features of the different nationalities."

Besides the above, I give a leader in the Times newspaper in London, in reference to the Peace Congress, which is characteristic of that paper to run down any such scheme.

"Mr. Cobden has been 'starring' in the Provinces during the week. It cannot be denied that, as far as numbers are concerned, he has drawn a numerous audience at Frankfort. The portion of his performance which appears to have given the most unlimited satisfaction, was the chaste and humorous manner in which he indoctrinated the motley assembly in the Paul's kirche in the mystery of a true British cheer. Henceforth it may be expected that the guttural sounds in which the chamois hunter of the Alps, and the green-coated rifleman of the Tyrolese mountains, are wont to give utterance to the pent-up emotions of their minds will give place to the measured 'hip,' 'hip,' 'hurrah!' of the Guild-Hall or Free-mason Tavern.

The remainder of Mr. Cobden's performance does not seem to have met with the same success, as his final point, nor is such consummation to be wondered at. A formidable rival sprung up in the person of an Ojibway Chief—who for the best portion of an hour indulged the audience with a rhapsody upon the impropriety of digging up the war hatchet—and taking a scalp from a fallen foe.

La Longue Calebine was the Jenny Lind of the Paul's kirche. He evidently got the better of Mr. Cobden, who to regain his ascendency could find nothing more to the purpose than to give the audience a sample of an English after-dinner cheer.

The people who had been collected together in the Paul's kirche were evidently delighted with the diversion after the weariness of the orators, and set about cheering with all the powers of their united lungs. To be sure there were no very subtle arguments to be deduced from their hurrahs, but they were, at any rate, as conclusive as the speeches.

Any serious comment upon the proceedings of the Peace meeting is entirely out of the question. One of the speakers—Mr. Hindley, of Oldham, had the *naïveté* to relate to the audience a short conversation between himself and Lord Brougham. The point of the anecdote was that Lord Brougham had once told M. Hindley that the ministers of the Peace Congress were 'the greatest fools.' Whatever our opinion may be, we might have hesitated before expressing it quite so tersely as the noble and learned Lord. But since the word has been said, we will only add that a great many people are of Lord Brougham's way of thinking upon this point. As to the horrors of warfare there can be no question. We have as profound a detestation of all armaments, military or naval, as the Ojibway Chief himself. We would hail with rapture the day when the last bayonet to be found in Europe was turned into a corkscrew or a carving-knife. But what avail our empty wishes? Is it right or honest to foster the delusion that any serious—any appreciable—influence over the course of events can be exercised by the delivery of a tissue of inane platitudes upon the advantages of peace and the calamities of war? It would be just as much to the purpose if a Congress should be held to-morrow to point out the beauties of truth, and the ugliness of lying. We do not see why each of the ten commandments should not in time furnish pretext for a meeting of nations in Frankfort or elsewhere. Charity, patience, humanity, honesty, sincerity, purity of word and deed, are all excellent topics for very excellent essays or orations. The human race requires to be set right upon each of these points to the full as much as upon the horrors of war. Nay, the series of ethical agitations we propose would be much more to the purpose, than what is called a Peace Congress. Mr. Cobden and the Ojibway are turning up a shallow furrow indeed. Could nations and individuals be persuaded to act with justice, and forbearance, and humanity,—could they be taught not to covet their neighbor's goods, and to do to others as they would themselves be done by, the armies of Europe might at once be put on the half-pay list. War is but the expression of evil passions—certainly on the side of one—probably on the part of both of the belligerent powers. But it would seem from the records of history that civilization is a plant of slow growth. Time is the great element in all human improvement. Men cannot be made just and merciful by a batch of speeches and in two or three hours' time.

When the present generation has passed away, and another and another, it may happen that the transcendental dreams of universal fraternity may be realized; but, as yet, we grieve to say it, we see little prospect for so desirable an object.

There is one point connected with the Congress which cannot but very forcibly arrest the attention. When we read over the resolutions proposed to the assembly we find them to consist as usual of recommendations of National disarmament, of disapprobation of foreign loans negotiated for the purpose of furnishing one people the means of slaughtering another, and so forth. Now, when these gentlemen find practically, that the governments of Europe cannot or will not disarm the troops at their command—when they see that, for all their talk, the Emperor of Russia need but propose a loan, and the subscription list is filled up in the course of a morning in the city—of what avail is it to persist in such visionary schemes? Whatever may be the case in days to come, the present Mr. Cobden and his Indian friend are before their age."

This is a fair specimen of English raillery which has been heard by us and read, as we have now travelled over a country which is now groaning in spite of its gigantic wealth.

It will be tolerated in other nations to say much against the Peace movement in this or any other country where less disaster has attended the passions of war—but an Englishman whose very country is now groaning of a debt created by the past folly of its Heads, is the last one who could be expected to say so much against the present benevolent movement of the cause of Peace.

The devastating effects of the national debt is felt in the splendid palaces of the rich, and reek in the gutters of the miserable. But, to be consistent—I have heard the Englishmen even say that the national debt was beneficial to the people! and to the country with its government. If this is beneficial—then the slavery entailed on the American continent by the British government in its early days must of course be a benefit to the people of this country. One is just as detestable as the other, and the present enlightened age will not tolerate such evils.

CHAPTER XIX.

VISIT TO HEIDELBERG.

SATURDAY morning, and a pleasant morning it is too. Our Congress is over, but the people are as busy as ever The Prince Frederick desired I should see him this morning at 7 o'clock, masonically. I saw him last evening just as he was leaving his room.

He is a fine-looking man, and as stately in his bearing as General Scott, of the United States. Indeed, I never saw a man more commanding in his appearance. This morning my friend Dr. J. W. Carove, desires me to visit the Heidelberg University, of which he is one of the Professors. After that, at 9 o'clock, I must bid farewell to the city of Frankfort.

As I was passing through the Parade Grounds the Prince was having a review of the soldiers. Ten thousand soldiers in arms! the sight was an imposing one. Their burnished weapons and splendid equipage glittered before the sun, and the tall plume of the Prince, who was conspicuous on the field, waved before us as we passed. These soldiers make a brilliant and formidable appearance, but such things are altogether repugnant to my feelings since my warrior's creed has been changed to a harmless one.

My visit to the University was pleasant. I ascended the Tower which is situated on a hill about three miles high, and had a panoramic view of the vast country which surrounds it. Far off in the westward are visible the peaks of the hills of France. A mountain range, looking as if its top was lost in the clouds, makes its appearance. The mountain on which I stood extended its rugged hill-tops northward, as far as the eye could reach. Far off in an easterly direction the villages of the German nation lay slumbering in peace and silence. There again rolls the tide of the beautiful Rhine. The fiery beams of the sun glisten on its surface, and the whole water appears as if it were a river of fire. Onward it rolls its winding course, its crystal waters enclosed in a locket of green. Here is also the Neckar, coming into sight as if it were just emerging from under the hill, and like a classic river of modern times it passes by this temple of learning. On the other side of the Neckar the farms appear in dots, and the whole valley is loaded with grain and vegetation. The hardy race of women are in the fields performing the duties of husbandmen, while their husbands, sons, and brothers are stationed at the frontier towns of the north, ready for war. These German women are short and portly and have ruddy complexions. With their sun-burnt faces they may compare to advantage, so far as redness is concerned, with any of our squaws in America; and like them they are serviceable at home and in the field. But of course there are *ladies* for the parlor in Germany as well as in every other civilized country. To grace saloons and drawing-rooms, women must be converted into butterflies, joined in the middle by a thread, ornamented with a great variety of hues, formed to flutter and fly about, and to live on sickening sweets, such as their counterparts, the flowers of the boudoir, may offer. There is more heart in a German peasant woman, and more soul in a simple-minded squaw, than in a thousand toys that are formed only for ornaments and playthings. Doubtless either extreme is to be deprecated, and the noble gentlewoman is a medium between the two, free from coarseness on the one hand and from frailty on the other.

The spires in the south-west are the steeples of Strausburg. I cannot stay here, for the time approaches when I must leave the town. I think of it with reluctance, and I shall be still more reluctant to part with these things which minister so greatly to my enjoyment. Where I stand it blows a gale, yet I would gladly stay here till sunset, and take a view of the surrounding scenery, the hills bathed in the glory of the setting sun, and the rich landscape softened by the shadows of the mountains. The whole valley is dotted with villages surrounded with vineyards and gardens that look as if they had been made for the lovers of the picturesque as much as for subsistence and comfort. Here and there the smoke rising from groups of dwellings, awaken a thousand associations of domestic peace and social harmony within, and, to one of great imagination, associations of fairy habitations, among the clouds. There is a rail-car coming up the valley! Its trail of smoke extending in a right line, and appearing motionless, while the car shoots over the ground like an arrow, produces a singular impression. The spinning of a fleece of black wool, is a homely comparison, but there might be a worse one.

The company who have managed to get up here are well pleased with the sight, and in accordance with custom I have recorded my name, nation, place of residence, &c. I must now descend and find my way to the University, to see the library, museum, and other objects of interest. But first of all I shall take a look at the old castld, which is the noblest ruin I ever beheld. I cannot do better than give the reader a description of it by one who knows something of its history.

"The Castle, anciently the residence of the Electors Palatine, presenting the combined character of a palace and a fortress, is an imposing ruin. The building displays the work of various hands, the taste of different founders, and the styles of successive centuries: it is highly interesting for its varied fortunes, its picturesque situation, its vastness, and the relics of architectural magnificence which it still displays, after having been three times burnt, and having ten times experienced the horrors of war. Its final ruin, however, did not arise from those causes; but after the greater part of the building had been restored to its former splendor in 1718–20, it was set on fire by lightning in 1764 : and since the total conflagration which ensued, it has never been rebuilt or tenanted. It is at present only a collection of red stone wall, and has remained roofless for nearly a century. It is approached by a carriage-road from behind, and by a winding foot-path on the side of the Neckar. The oldest part remaining is probably that built by the Electors Rudolph and Rupert. It has all the character of a stronghold of the middle ages, and the teeth of the portcullis still project from beneath the archway leading to it. The Friedrichsbau, named from the Elector, who built it in 1607, is distinguished by excessive richness of decoration : its façade to the south is ornamented with statues of ancestors of the electoral family from Charlemagne. The part of the building most deserving of admiration, for the good taste of its design, and the elegance of its decorations, is that which overlooks the river, and extends along the east side of the quadrangle built by Otto Henry (1556), in the style called cinque cento, which is allied to the Elizabethan of England. The statues of heroes from sacred and profane history, which decorate the front, though of (keuper) sandstone, are by no means contemptible as works of art.

The English traveller will view with some interest that part of the castle called the English Palace, from its having been built for the reception of the Princess Elizabeth Stuart, daughter of James I., and granddaughter of Mary Queen of Scots. The triumphal arch, having pillars entwined with ivy leaves, was erected by her husband, the Elector Frederick V., afterwards King of Bohemia, to celebrate their nuptials; it led to the flower-garden which he caused to be laid out for her pleasure, and it still goes by the name of Elizabethan Pforte.

"When her husband hesitated to accept the crown of Bohemia, this high-hearted wife exclaimed, 'Let me rather eat dry bread at a king's table than feast at the board of an elector:' and it seemed as if some avenging demon hovered in the air, to take her literally at her word; for she and her family lived to eat dry bread—ay, and to beg it before they ate it; but she *would* be a queen."—Mrs. Jameson. The granite pillars supporting the canopy of the well in the corner of the court of the castle are said by some to have been brought from Charlemagne's palace at Ingelheim, though they are undoubtedly derived from the quarry in the Odenwald.

In a cellar under the castle is the famous Heidelberg Tun; it is the largest wine cask in the world, being capable of holding 800 hogsheads, or 283,200 bottles, which is far less, after all, than the dimensions of the porter vat of a London brewer. In former days, when the Tun was filled with the produce of the vintage, it was usual to dance on the platform on the top. It has, however, remained empty since 1769, more than half a century.

One of the towers which formed the outer defences of the Castle (*der Gesprengte Thurm*) was undermined and blown up by the French; but so thick were the walls, and so strongly built, that though nearly the whole of one side was detached by the explosion, instead of crumbling to pieces, it merely slid down from its place, in one solid mass, into the ditch, where it still remains. Subterranean passages, for the most part still preserved and accessible, extend under the ramparts.

The Gardens and Shrubberies round the castle, and the adjoining Terrace, to the eastward, afford the most agreeable walks and splendid points of view it is possible to conceive over the Neckar, issuing out of its vine-clad valley, and winding through a plain of the utmost fertility to join the Rhine, which appears here and there in distant flashes glittering in the sun. Spires and towers proclaim the existence of cities and villages almost without number, and the landscape is bounded by the outline of the Vosges mountains.

The best general view of the building may be obtained from the extremity of the terrace raised upon arches, and prejecting over the Neckar. The castle, however, is so grand an object, and the surrounding country so exceedingly beautiful, that the stranger will hardly be satisfied with seeing it from one point. He should mount the heights on the right bank of the Neckar, either by a path leading from the end of the bridge, which is steep, or by a more gradual ascent from Neuenheim. An agreeable path, easily accessible, called the Philosopher's Walk, conducts along the slope of the hill fronting the town. The hill behind it, which stands in the angel between the valley of the Rhine and Neckar, called the Heiligeberg, presents a more extensive prospect. On the top are ruins of a castle and church of St. Michael, which succeeded to a Roman fort built on the spot. In 1391, the sect called Flaggellants made a pilgrimage to this holy mountain, clad in black, and wearing a white cross in front and behind. In the thirty years' war, Tilly opened his trenches to bombard the town from this point.

About 50 yards above the bridge, on the right bank, in a solitary inn called Hirschgasse, the students' duels are fought. Four or five sometimes take place in a day; and it is no uncommon thing for a student to have been engaged in 25 or 30, *as principal*, in the course of four or five years.

The Konigstsuhl, the highest hill in this district, lies behind the town and castle. The summit may be reached in 1, or 1½ hour's walk, and the view is the most extensive in the neighborhood. A lofty tower has been erected for the convenience of visitors, who often repair hither to see the sun rise, and if possible to extend the limits of the panorama, which includes the valleys of the Rhine and Neckar, the Odenwald, Haardt Mountains on the W., the Taunus on the N. W., the ridge of the Black Forest on the S., with the castle of Ebersteinburg, near Baden, and the spire of Strasburg Minster, 90 miles off. Tilly bombarded the town from this hill, after his attack from the right bank, and failed: remains of his trenches are still visible.

There is a small tavern near the top, called Kohlhof, where persons anxious to see the sun rise sometimes pass the night previously.

The banks of the Neckar above Heidelberg are very interesting, and afford many pleasant excursions—one of the most agreeable being to Neckargemünd (Inn, Pfalz; good), six miles off.

A road, overlooking the Neckar, runs from the castle, along the shoulder of the hill to the Wolf's Brunnen, an agreeable walk of two miles. It is a pretty retired nook, named from a spring which rises there. There is a small inn close to it, famed for its trout."

Here I saw a ceremony of embracing, which I never saw before in any country. Dr. Pennington, an American delegate for the colored race, having once been made a D.D., and received a diploma from the Professors of this Institution, met for the first time some of the Professors; and a Dr., one of the Professors, having been informed that Mr. Pennington was among the strangers who had come to visit the University, immediately sought for him, and they met in the old dilapidated chapel inside of the old castle. They made addresses for the crowd first, and then they embraced one another before the audience, and *kissed each other*. While I was looking for some corner in which I might indulge my pardonable smile, I stumbled over an old dried up monk with his hands outstretched towards me for *alms*. It was, however, only an image clothed in rags.

The library is a wonderful collection of books and MSS., both ancient and modern. Here we saw Luther's MS., a "Dissertation on the Prophecies of Isaiah," and his "Exhortation to Prayer against the Turks," and other momentos of him in different forms.

The time is now over, and I am required to return to Frankfort, just in time for the cars! On my left is seated my warm-hearted friend, Dr. J. W. Crovae. Weary, and my eyes filled with dust, I fell asleep. Dreamed of *home*—O, how provoking!

When we took leave of Frankfort this morning, we left a German with a pipe in his mouth, standing near the station, pointing the passengers to another part of the building. This afternoon he is here still, standing in the same place, and smoking the same identical pipe, though it is probable that a number of pipes full of tobacco have passed into smoke since morning. In most cases useless and noxious things, however much they may be favorites of the public, end in smoke. This is a fair specimen of the smoking propensity of the Germans.

August 27th. I have visited a place of resort near Weisbaden, the prettiest I have seen. It is a gambling place, authorized by the government; and all ranks (it would not be proper to say *classes*), of the people go there —ladies as well as gentlemen. I stood in the hall a few minutes ago, and saw a file of men and women, 15 or 20 in number, standing with their florins in hand and throwing them into a pile, when a single toss would tell the story whether they gained or lost. One man had 25 florins in his hand, and threw one at a time until he had but two left, and those two won him back what he had thrown upon the table and seven florins besides. The players sat opposite each other, with faces as hard as marble, and hearts still harder, no doubt.

But the gardens, walks, lakes, fountains, are all beautiful. This city is the prettiest I have seen in this country, without any exception.

The 28th, I leave for Dusseldorf to visit the German poet, Mr. Freiligrath.

At 9 o'clock, I am on the Rhine, gliding along in a swift steamer. O, how delightful! The hill-tops turning about as we pass them by, as if to present themselves to us in every position, that we may take a view of them on all sides. The passengers are all on deck, gazing as if it were the first time. There are, however, a few exceptions. For the thousandth time you exclaim, " What a difference there is in people !" There is a man from —— who seems not to know that there is anything to admire in the scenery around him. In his hands is a novel, and his soul, if he has one, is wrapped up in that. It is not merely every creature that has four legs that is an animal. If any of my own acquaintance were to fix their eyes on a book when passing over such a beautiful country as this, I would jerk their heads up at the risk of offending them, and tell them to see the glorious attire with which nature adorns herself.

I enjoyed the trip coming down much better than that going up, for there were not so many passengers on board.

My friend Mr. Close accompanied me to Dusseldorf, where I find the famous poet, who, on account of his republican feelings and predilections is not allowed to publish his poems without inspection by the government. For the violation of this rule he has seen the inside of a prison—of such a tolerant character is the government of Prussia!

Him and his Turkish lady I find very affable and kind. Both are handsome, and their minds are as good as, yea better, than their looks. A lovely little pappoose, a picture of innocence, lies nestling in a cradle. Bud of promise, unfolding thy tender leaves to the scorching heats, the biting frosts, and the merciless storms of this world, take this kiss from a red man of the American wilderness. Thou hast a softer bed, and more tender hands to rear thee, in this garden of the Old World, than the wild flower that buds and blossoms in the forests of the New. For thy own and thy parents' sake, God bless thee, sweet babe!

My time being limited, I leave for Cologne, where I expect to spend the evening with men of science.

About half a dozen of us spend the evening together, and endeavor to amuse each other. Students from Bonn arrived about 12 o'clock. My friends have been trying very hard to make me drink. Though this is a very strange way of showing their friendship, they are nevertheless friends—such inconsistencies do the customs of society subject us to!

To their *cordial* solicitations I said "no," but finding they "would not take *no* for an answer," I left the company rather unceremoniously, about 2 o'clock in the morning. At an early hour I found they had been hunting for me through the crooked and coffin-like streets of Cologne until 4 o'clock, or daylight. They thought, I suppose, that an *Indian* could not find his way home.

For a literary and scientific people these Germans are a strange set. Their recreations are in proportion to their soundness and laboriousness as scholars. Among other things which they learn they will find that when I say *yes* I mean *yes*, and when I say *no* I mean *no*—according to the scripture injunction, "Let your yea be yea and your nay nay."

While speaking of this celebrated poet I here give a short notice of him, and a piece of exquisite poetry, from his pen :—

"One of the most gifted of modern German poets is Freiligrath, the author of the exquisite poem we copy below. His early education was a commercial one, having served his time as a clerk in a wealthy banking house of Holland. He secretly cultivated poetry, while immersed in business occupations; and, unknown to his friends, began to contribute to a German periodical the first fledgelings of his genius. Among his earliest productions was the poem subjoined, which immediately attracted great attention, and won golden opinions for the author. Freiligrath soon left his commercial pursuits, which were always distasteful to him, and took to literature for his profession. Among those who first discovered and appreciated his genius was the King of Prussia, who, finding upon inquiry that he was dependent upon his pen for a support, offered him a yearly salary, which would place him above want. Freiligrath availed himself of this salary, however, but a year or two. At heart a liberal, he could not honestly accept the patronage of a monarch whose policy he could never approve, and, throwing up this salary, he fearlessly joined the liberal party, and published the celebrated volume of political poems called 'Glaubensbekentrisse,' which were no sooner issued than they were confiscated, and he was obliged to fly the land. He went to England, and there engaged as a corresponding clerk in a commercial house, until the revolution in Germany broke out. He then returned to Düsseldorf, where he was for a long time imprisoned, under pretence of causing a demonstration against the King of Prussia. He was soon liberated, however, and has since, we believe, returned to England.

Freiligrath married a very beautiful and accomplished Greek lady, and is the father of two or three lovely children. We understand that he is intending a visit to America, to locate himself if possible here, as a Professor in some one of our universities. Americans should take him cordially by the hand, and we are sure that a professional chair could by no one be better, or more worthily filled.

On the soft cushions of a couch of down
Slumbers the maid, imprisoned in repose;
Close droop her eyelashes, profuse and brown;
Her cheek is tinted like a full-blown rose.

Hard by there shimmers in the smothered light
A vase of choicest ornament and mould;
And in the vase are fresh-cut flowers, and bright,
Fragrant to smell, and various to behold.

Damp are the heats that, broodingly and dull,
Flow and flow on throughout the chamber small;
Summer has scared away the tender cool,
Yet fastened stand the casements one and all.

Stillness around, and deepest silence lowers;
Suddenly, hark! a whisper as of CHANGE;
Heard in the tender stems, heard in the flowers,
It lisps and nestles eagerly and strange.

Swing from the cups that tremble on those stems
  The little spirits, the embodied scents,
Some bearing shields, some topped with diadems,
  Delicate mists their robe and ornaments.

From the flushed bosom of the queenly Rose
  Arises gracefully a slender Lady,
Pearls glisten in her hair, that freely flows
  As dew-drops glisten where the copse is shady.

Forth from the visor of the "Helmet plant"
  A keen-faced Knight steps mid the dark-green leaves,
His presence breathing high chivalric vaunt;
  Complete in steel he shines from crest to greaves;

Over his morion, nodding waywardly,
  Hangs heron plumage, gray, and silver pale,
Leaving the "Lily," with sick, languid eye,
  A wood-nymph, thin as gossamer her veil.

Out of the "Turk-cap" comes a swarthy Moor,
  Wearing his flaunting robes with scornful show;
On his green turban glitters, fixed before,
  The golden radiance of the crescent bow.

Forth from the "Crown Imperial," bold and tall,
  Sceptre in hand, appears an ermined King;
From the blue "Iris," girt with falchions all,
  His hunters troop, green-vested like the spring.

Sullenly swirling down from the "Narciss,"
  A youthful form, with silent sorrow laden,
Steps to the bed, to print his fevered kiss
  Upon the red lips of the sleeping maiden.

The other spirits, crowding, press and swing
All round the couch in many circles gay;
They swing and press themselves, and softly sing
Over the sleeper their mysterious lay:—

"Maiden, O cruel maiden! thou hast torn
Up from the earth our every slender tie,
And, in this gaudy-colored shard forlorn,
Left us to weaken, wither, fade, and die.

"Alas! how happy once was our repose
On the maternal bosom of the earth,
Where through the tall tree-tops that o'er us rose,
The sun made vistas to behold our mirth!

"The balmy spring, with many a gentle breeze,
Cooled our weak stems that to its bidding bent
At eve descending under the still trees
How blissful was our faery merriment!

"Clear on us then fell heaven's own dew and rain;
Foul water now surrounds us stagnantly
We fade, and we shall die—but not in vain,
If, ere we pass, our vengeance lights on thee."

The spirits' song is hushed, their errand told;
Bending, around the sleeper's couch they go;
And, with the brooding silences of old,
Returns again the whispering soft and low.

Hark! how the rustling rises round the wreath!
How glow her cheeks, instinctive of their doom!
See how upon her all the spirits breathe—
How the scents undulate throughout the room!

The slanted sparkles of the western day
  Smiting the room, each spirit vanisheth ;
Upon the cushions of the couch she lay ;
  As beautiful and, ah ! as cold as death.

One faded blossom, lying all alone,
  Lends to her cheek a tender tint of red,
With her wan sisters sleeps that hapless one—
  Oh ! fatal breath of flowers !—the maid is dead. H. G. K.

They had agreed to meet and accompany me to the station for Calais, at 6½ o'clock, but only one was present to bid me farewell. I am now again on my way to Calais, and London.

Travelled all day and all night—the road dusty, and our company quite jaded—a poorer-looking set I never saw—passed over Dover, Brighton, and Conlay—I am in London again

CHAPTER XX.

LONDON AGAIN.

I HAVE just got inside of Babylon again. The noise and confusion which reign over this great city, would make stronger heads than mine to turn and ache. "Buses" long and narrow, low and humiliating, and affectionately close. There are but the lower classes who has monopolized these in this country, and very seldom any of the higher classes are even seen in them. There are a great many thousand of these conveniences which run from the Exchange, London Bridge, and the great thoroughfares of the city. There are in general twenty-one for a load. Thirteen inside and eight outside, and sometimes more than enough.

The peculiar feature in the appearance of the stores in the oldest part of London is the narrowness of its stores, which is generally the case in the famous street Cheapside. But in the west end, the resort of the upper-ten-dom, the stores are more of a modern size and appearance. Particularly so in Regent street. There are stores there which in point of richness surpass anything I have ever seen. The stores in New York are some as neat-looking as any I have seen. Nothing of all that I have seen surpasses in point of size, convenience, elegance of taste, as that one in New York lately built by "Bowen & McNamee," their extensive silk store, and that of Stewart's.

The streets are generally narrow in the old part of the city. Long, crooked, high and dark, dismal, smutty-looking after a gas-light is very soon after that necessary to travel with. Or if no gas-light, a man must accustom himself to walking by faith, or feeling.

I have to officiate in the Rev. Mr. Luke's Chapel Sunday twice. As he is still on the continent. A delightful audience. An attentive one. And I should judge an intelligent one also.

The people here call their meeting-houses of all Dissenters, Chapels, and the Established Churches are only to be called a Church or Churches.

The Chapels and Churches that I have been in, in this city, are very old fashioned. No cushioned seats, high backs, and one sitting in them can sleep very easy, and not a sight of anything except your head.

The pulpits are more like a barrel, and when shown in one of these I always did feel as though I was in a barrel hooped-up and was speaking through a bunghole,—standing in one position,—there is therefore no animation. Not much elbow-room, neither for the feet. Cramped on all sides, one cannot but wish for room. I know it is not necessary with some to have any room, and others again—that is the most effective part of their performance.

Monday morning. I had a visit from a gentleman and lady who offer me a suite of rooms. And I am glad that the Great Spirit has put this into their hearts, as to do me this kindness. I have gladly availed myself of seeing them early in this week.

Found cards in my room of people who have called. I *must* go to this and to that one. I cannot go to all, my time is limited, and however pleased I might be to see them, some like myself must be disappointed.

To record the events of this week would be to commence another volume, when I have spent the most agreeable part of my sojourn in England.

Letters after letters. This morning I received at a quarter before 9 o'clock eighteen letters! And two committees have waited on me, for to go and deliver addresses to their people, for objects of Benevolence.

I had expected a great deal might be done to do some good to my own countrymen in the way of presenting the object of their own educational interests, and for this reason I endeavored to seek the aid and countenance of the so-called "Aboriginal Protection Society"—and instead of being any benefit I had to just leave off everything when so many obstacles were thrown in my way.

I had made a false high estimation of this body. A great name indeed without any power. A body without a knowing aim, and less energy of purpose.

I see a Quaker friend from Philadelphia is also here in the city, presenting his colonization scheme, in which very few of the people seem to interest themselves.

In the visits that I made with a Rev. Gentleman in the poor districts of this great city I find much misery and wretchedness.

Another afternoon has been allotted to visiting the Ragged schools. Certainly it is not a poetical name. These schools are poor-looking enough, but certainly they looked a great deal better than names indicated. Delivered five addresses to-day, and endeavored to please and gratify the young English boys and girls. God bless them.

I have now delayed over two weeks in this city, and having received an invitation to go to Scotland and from Lord Brougham at his country-seat, I leave now for Leeds.

The travel between here and that city is very good; and everything comfortable.

Here I stayed for a short time and delivered addresses to the sabbath-school children in one of the churches. Preached on Sabbath, lectured on week days, and visited during the day the surrounding country.

This is a great manufacturing country. Cloth is here made to perfection. I have just visited Mr. Rawson's cloth factory, where I have seen the process of cloth-making.

Here the railways meet from all directions—diverging over the whole surrounding country.

I used to read a great deal about Leeds.

To look over it from the highest hill near-by appears as if it was one vast smoke house. Smoke, smoke, all but smoke.

The consul of the United States here is a fine hearted gentleman.

In my visit to this place I found the historical notices of this place as follows, which I hope will be of some use to my readers in the way of information :

" Leeds, the largest and most flourishing town of Yorkshire, on the Aire, is the metropolis of the woollen manufacture, and the fifth town in England in point of population and commercial activity. It is an ancient town, and was probably a Roman station, but has been the scene of no historical events. Its situation is highly advantageous for manufacturing and commercial purposes. The chief articles of manufacture here are superfine cloths, kerseymeres, swansdowns, shalloons, carpets, blankets, &c. ; plate-glass, earthenware, and the spinning of flax to a great extent. Its merchants also buy extensively the woollen and stuff goods made in the neighboring towns and villages, and get them finished and dyed ; so that Leeds is a general mart for all these fabrics. The Leeds cloth-halls form an interesting spectacle on the market-days. Machine-making is a flourishing business in Leeds. The Leeds and Liverpool Canal connects Leeds with the Western sea, and by means of the river

Aire it has a communication with the Humber. By means of railways, this town now enjoys every advantage which can be given, by the most rapid communication with all parts of Great Britain. Leeds has eight churches, numerous dissenting chapels, a free grammar school, a national school, a philosophical and literary society, a mechanics' institute, a theatre, and various charitable institutions. Leeds was the native place of Dr. Hartley, author of Observations on Man; Wilson, the painter; and Smeaton, the celebrated engineer. Dr. Priestley, the distinguished philosopher, officiated for several years as the minister of the Unitarian chapel here. Leeds gives the title of Duke to the family of Osborne, which sprung from this town. Two M.P. Pop. of town and liberty, 152,054.

About three miles from Leeds are the ruins of Kirkstall Abbey, picturesquely situated in a vale watered by the Aire. This abbey was founded in 1157 by Henry de Lacy for monks of the Cistertian order."

CHAPTER XXI.

FIRST VISIT TO SCOTLAND.

HAVING always had a great desire to visit the country of the Scots, I must leave Leeds and travel northward with my son and lady, and see the famed country so much honored with the songs of the two best poets in their day—Robert Burns and Sir Walter Scott.

On our journey we go first to see the birthplace of my companion in Knaresborough; and after visiting Ripon at the residence of Mr. William Hovell, the brother of my father-in-law. The numerous curiosities here in Knaresborough are interesting. I visited the Dropping Well, and wrote my notices a few steps where the water drips. Thus is a romantic wilderness connected with all the scenery of this stream of water which rolls along so silently here. Rock, bold, and large trees overhanging their branches are standing along the rugged banks—and here cool breezes assemble and run in ripples over the smooth surface of the clear waters of this singular spot.

How often did I use to hear in Canada from a portly fair one of this place. The walks, yea, the moonlight walks, as the silent waters rolled underneath in the deep shade of yon valley. Step after step, then the waters descend from the wood-hill, it emerges and then sunning itself in clear noonday—where the lamb and the herds of the tame ones are sporting over the fields made green by its waters.

The Town Hall is a wretched place. I deliver an address in the Hall, and find some warm hearts here for all it does look rather forlorn just now. A railroad runs by the town.

I give here the historical notices of the place :

" Knaresborough is delightfully situated on the banks of the Nidd, which flows through a most romantic valley below precipitous rocks. The church is a large old structure, containing several monuments. Here are the remains of a castle which was erected soon after the conquest. It belonged at one time to Piers Gaveston, the favorite of Edward II. In the year 1331 it was granted by Edward III. to his son, the celebrated John of Gaunt, and was afterwards one of the places in which Richard II. was imprisoned. During the civil wars it sustained a siege from the parliamentary forces under Lord Fairfax, and at last surrendered upon honorable terms. It was afterwards dismantled by order of the parliament. Part of the principal tower is still remaining. In the walk along the bank of the Nidd opposite the ruins of the castle, is a celebrated petrifying or dropping well, springing in a declivity at the foot of a limestone rock. Near it is a curious excavation called St. Robert's Chapel, hollowed out of the solid rock; its roof is groined, and the altar adorned with Gothic ornaments. About half a mile lower down the river are the remains of a priory founded by Richard Plantagenet. A mile to the east is St. Robert's cave, remarkable on account of the discovery of a skeleton here in 1759, which led to the conviction and execution of the celebrated Eugene Aram. Knaresborough has manufactories of linen and cotton, and its corn-market is one of the largest in the county. Two M P. Pop. 4,678. Knaresborough was the birthplace of the famous blind guide John Metcalf. He had lost his sight in infancy, and yet frequently acted as a guide over the forest during the night, or when the paths were covered with snow,—contracted for making roads, building bridges, &c. He died in 1810, aged ninety-three years."

I visited to-day the town of Harrogate. Placed in a level land, and surrounded with hedges, houses rather scattered. It is the Saratoga of the county of Yorkshire. There are thousands here now to drink the water. The mineral springs which are found here is all that which has builded this town—and boarding-houses are as numerous as any of the Spa places in America.

They charge all they can get too, and they will not refuse even any amount after you have paid your bill.

The Brunswick House is very good, but we rather liked the "Crown Hotel," where they charged us an aristocratic charge for four days.

Here is the historical notice of it—short and brief. We have had some good times here, friends are kind, and attended my lectures well:

"Harrogate is celebrated for its mineral springs, which are annually visited by about 2,000 persons. It consists of two scattered villages, known by the names of High and Low Harrogate, situated about a mile from each other, and possessing ample accommodation for visitors. Harrogate possesses both chalybeate and sulphurous springs. Of the former the oldest is the Tewit Well, which was discovered about the year 1576. The Old Spa, situated on the Stray, was discovered by Dr. Stanhope, previous to 1631. The Starbeck chalybeate is about midway between Harrogate and Knaresborough. The Saline chalybeate is situated at Low Harrogate, and was discovered in 1819. The sulphurous springs are, the Old Sulphur Wells, situated at Low Harrogate, close by the Leeds and Ripon road ; the Crown Sulphur Well, situated in the pleasure-grounds belonging to the Crown Hotel; and the Knaresborough or Starbeck Spa, situated nearly midway between Harrogate and Knaresborough. Harrogate possesses a considerable number of hotels, several boarding-houses, public baths, promenade-rooms, ball and billiard-rooms, circulating libraries and reading-rooms, four places of worship, &c. High and Low Harrogate contain upwards of 4,000 inhabitants."

Saturday morning we set off to the North, to the great coal place, Newcastle-upon-Tyne.

The railroad leads over a quite level country. Farms, towns, and gentlemen's country-seats, are on our left and on our right. The sky is better here. Coal-pits are all along each side of the road. And vast quantities of coal lay in heaps just from the bowels of the earth.

Newcastle is a very interesting city; I preached here, and always had very full audiences, and to Mr. McLiver I am indebted for this, and afterwards also, from my warm-hearted friend, Joseph Kimpster, one of the Delegates to the Peace Congress.

The notices of this place are given as follows:

"Newcastle-upon-Tyne is supposed to have derived its origin from Pons Ælii, the second station from the eastern extremity of the Roman wall. Previous to the Conquest the place was called Monkchester, from the number of monastic institutions; its present name was derived from a castle erected here by Robert, eldest son of William the Conqueror, on his return from an expedition into Scotland. Newcastle was anciently the resort of numerous pilgrims, who came to visit the holy well of Jesus' Mount, now Jesmond, a mile north-east of the town. One of the principal streets in Newcastle is still called Pilgrim Street. Another ancient town, called Pampedon, appears to have been included in the limits of the modern Newcastle; its name may be traced in the modern Pandon Hall, Pandon Bank, &c. Newcastle has been the scene of many most interesting events in the history of England. David I. of Scotland made himself master of the town in the reign of Stephen, and obliged the people to swear allegiance to the Empress Maude. Here John of England and William the Lion of Scotland had a conference in the year 1209. Here again Alexander of Scotland and his Queen came, in 1235–36, and had a conference with the King of England. Here John Baliol did homage to Edward I. for the crown of Scotland. In 1293, the famous Sir William Wallace, in one of his inroads into England, made several vehement but unsuccessful attacks upon the town. In 1318, during the reign of Edward II., an unsuccessful attempt at a permanent peace between the Scots and English was made here—two nuncios from the Pope, and two envoys from Philip of France, besides the English and Scotch commissioners, being present. In 1342, David Bruce, King of Scotland, made an unsuccessful attack upon the town shortly before the battle of Neville's Cross; and, twelve years afterwards, commissioners met here to consult on his ransom. In 1642, Newcastle was besieged by the Scottish army under General Lesley; but the Marquis of Newcastle, who was governor for the King, successfully defended the town against him. In the next year, however, the Scots under General Leven took it by storm; but Sir John Marley, then mayor, retired to the castle, with about 500 men, which he held till terms of capitulation were obtained. In 1636, above 5,000 persons died of the plague at Newcastle. In 1646, Charles I. was brought hither from Newark by the Scots, to whom he had surrendered himself. Newcastle is supposed to have been incorporated by William Rufus; but the first mayor was appointed in the reign of Henry III.

The town, which has more than doubled its size during the present century, is situated on the summit and declivities of three lofty eminences, rising from the north bank of the Tyne, and ten miles from its mouth. The town of Gateshead occupies the opposite bank, and may be regarded as a sort of suburb of Newcastle. "A strange mixture of ancient and modern objects strikes your eye in the more lofty and prominent features of Newcastle. There stands, tall, and stalwart, and square, and black as ink, the old donjon-keep of Robert Curthose, the son of the Conqueror. To the left still higher towers over the town the fine steeple of St. Nicholas, and to the right the new and lofty column in honor of Earl Grey. Here, along the banks of the river, you see ranges, one above another, of dim and dingy buildings, that have stood for centuries amid the smoke of the great capital of coal; and there, on its bold eminence, a Grecian fabric, standing proudly aloft, like the Temple of Minerva in Athens. Beyond it, again, you catch the tops of houses, and ranges of streets, that indicate a degree of modern magnificence which at once astonishes you in the midst of so much that is different, and stimulates you to a nearer inspection."*

Newcastle has undergone a most wonderful change during the last few years. In the centre of the town the old and narrow streets have been swept away, and some of the noblest and most magnificent streets and squares in the kingdom erected in their room. The person by whose genius and industry this marvellous change has been effected is Mr. Grainger, a native of the town, who has made his way from the condition of a charity boy, and the apprentice to a carpenter and builder. "The following," says Miss Martineau, "is a summary of five years' work of Mr. Grainger, from August, 1834, to August, 1839. The old property removed consisted of

* Howitt's Visits to Remarkable Places, 2d Series, p. 287.

two theatres, the late butcher-market, Anderson Place, one large inn, eight public-houses, eighty private houses, and a great number of work-shops and inferior buildings. The site of the improvements cost £145,937, workmen's wages and materials, £499,753 ; total, £645,690. Out of this have arisen the following : nine new streets, extending collectively 1 mile 289 yards ; the new market, the central exchange, new theatre, new dispensary, music hall, lecture room, two chapels, Incorporated Company's Hall, two auction marts, ten inns, twelve public-houses, forty private houses, and 325 houses with shops. The value of the whole amounts to £995,000." Besides these magnificent erections, Mr. Grainger's plan comprehends the junction of several railways, the formation of extensive quays, the erection of ranges of manufactories, and on the high ground of villas and terraces.

The other objects of interest in Newcastle are St. Nicholas' Church, a handsome edifice, with a beautiful spire in the form of an imperial crown, an altar-piece, by Tintoretto, and a valuable library, containing, among other curious books, the Bible of Hexham Abbey ;—St. Andrew's Church, a very ancient structure, part of it of Norman architecture—St. John's Church, containing an ancient font and several ancient monuments; All Saints' Church, a modern edifice of Grecian architecture, with a steeple 202 feet high; St. Ann's, St. Thomas's, Mary Magdalene, &c.; the infirmary, the Keelmen's Hospital, the monument erected to Earl Grey, surmounted by a statue of that nobleman; the Royal Arcade, 250 feet long, by 20 wide and 35 feet high, &c. The new covered market is pronounced to be the finest in the kingdom. Its area is more than two acres. Newcastle also possesses several meeting-houses, hospitals, and other charitable institutions, a literary and scientific institution, containing a fine library and reading room, a museum room of Egyptian antiquities, a gallery of Roman altars, and other antiquities, &c. The free grammar school was founded by Thomas Horsley, who was mayor of Newcastle in 1525. Here the late Lords Eldon, Stowell, and Collingwood, the poet Akenside, and other eminent persons received the earlier part of their education.

The principal business of Newcastle is in the shipment of coals, the produce of the surrounding coal-pits. About three millions of tons of coals are shipped annually from the river Tyne. The other chief articles of export are lead, cast and wrought iron, glass and pottery, copperas and other chemical productions, soap, colors, grindstones, salt, and pickled salmon. The imports are wine, spirituous liquors, and fruit, corn, timber, flax, tallow, and hides from the Baltic, and tobacco and various other articles from North America.

Newcastle returns two members to Parliament. Pop. 49,860."

Newcastle is a noted place, and of late the railway king, George Hudson, has done some good to this town by having an iron and stone bridge which has been placed across the chasm that forms the winding of the river. A beautiful piece of workmanship it is too.

A white man, a day or two ago, deliberately took off his clothes on the top of this bridge and jumped down to the water just for the amusement of the bystanders—after coming up, he took up a collection among the witnesses to his performance.

Good as this place is, and kind as the friends are to us, we must travel still northward, to Edinburgh.

The railroad scuds over the country which perceptibly begins to change into a mountainous region from a low monotonous country, yea, the road leads over a beautiful country, just by precipices nearly overhanging the sea-shore. On one side is the mountain region, on the other is the ocean sweeping on its bosom a thousand ships, and far off is a steamer like a mere speck in the ocean. Its snake-like trail behind hangs and is lost in the clear sky from behind.

Though I have letters of some importance, yet I cannot find it so convenient to be dependent altogether to great names as long as one can help himself.

And now we are in Edinburgh! the great city of the Scotch people. This is that Castle which often I have heard about, and now recurs to me a scene which I saw some years ago in my native land. It was a group of Scotch people who had just settled near by my father's. Just then I began to hear them speak, and I heard the name Edinburgh, and Edinburgh Castle so often that I could speak it, if I could nothing besides—for an elderly woman with a pipe in her hand was sitting in the corner of the log-fire, and she in speaking of "Edinburgh Castle," wept like a child. "Na, na, na, ever see Edinburgh Castle," said she, as she shook her head into her lap.

I love to see in any one a love of country, so much as to weep at the mention of one's birthplace.

And this is the city of palaces, and there are a great many things to admire in this city. It is situated in a romantic and abrupt country—high, naked hills,—grim-visaged, hard-browed, and frowning with dignity. And amidst this country so full of hills and so full of valleys is this city situated. There is yonder palace where the Queen of Scots lived, "Holyrood Palace," and on that high hill is the Edinburgh Castle, in which King James was born.

O what lovely sight it is to see in this wild scene monuments to the memory of Scott and Burns! I can hardly see Nelson's on account of these others.

I traversed this city, and saw a great many good men—the Rev. William Ried, one of the most eloquent divines of this country, and a go-a-head reformer. Noble and generous. God bless his heart. I spend a part of a week here and the other in Glasgow, and I might stay here all the rest of my days among a people who seem to be so full of kindness.

I delivered three lectures in Edinburgh and two in Glasgow, and finding I am required to be in London at the first great meeting of the people who are friendly to the cause of Temperance, I must again repair to London.

While I stayed in Edinburgh I met J. P. Nichols, LL.D., with whom I found much interest, as he has been in America, and spoke much in favor of the Americans as a kind-hearted race of people.

I took breakfast with Professor Simpson, the discoverer of chloroform, near the sea-shore with other friends. A man of middle age, stature full, and rather in the aldermanic order, his face well-proportioned,—and his forehead indicates his acquired fame.

The strangest thing that I saw was the fossil tree, the remains of a tree in the rock under the hill of stone, which, in blasting for rocks they found in a state of preservation, having turned into a rock. There it still lay perfect—its roots—and branches, and tapered-off somewhat inclined.

This is about 25 or 30 feet under the hill, and a short distance from the water. No one can tell how long this may have lain here.

After speaking to crowded houses in Edinburgh and Glasgow, I must leave for London, by the way of Berwick.

And after a travel of a day and a half I am again in London.

CHAPTER XXII.

LECTURES AND ADDRESSES IN LONDON, AND TRAVELS TO THE NORTH.

THE great meeting at the London Tavern is over, and the papers are full of notices of it. Some applaud and some condemn the speeches.

It was a brilliant sight indeed. Crowds had to leave for want of room.

I will sit down and write about it to one of the Boston papers—of things in general which I have seen, and what I have done in my northern tour.

LONDON, Oct. 25th, 1850.

EDITORS NEW-ENGLANDER :—

Though I have been very silent since I came to this country, it is not that I have been idle.

After enjoying the tour through Germany, Holland and Belgium, I came to the city of London, and have been travelling in the North of England for five weeks, and

13*

saw a glimpse of the Highlands of Scotland. I must say, with reference to the home of the noble-hearted Scotch, it is near like the grandeur of America Ours is of course better.

In my tour to the North, I have delivered lectures in the principal cities and towns on my way, which were well attended. I found in Newcastle-upon-Tyne a very warm reception, and when I came away felt as though I was leaving my only friends. I hope to see them again.

In Scotland I found a people sturdy, energetic, enterprising; and in Edinburgh I can say I have friends who will always be in the right place in my heart. Here-and-there I have delivered temperance lectures for the people, and though, in this land of "drinking," one has to have an unusual precaution not to be led by the popular fashion of drinking; for if any one is to dine with lords and dukes, there it is temperance principles are to be tested. Comparing this country with America, the latter is a sober country, for here, beer-drinking and gin-drinking are the bane. The English are a beer-drinking nation,—the Scotch, a whiskey-drinking nation,—and the French, a wine-drinking nation. Each of these, of course, drink other drinks besides cold water, but it is the above peculiar drinks in which *each excels.* And yet, through England and Scotland the people are at work in organizing societies for the prevention of this bane of civilization.

In Scotland, I addressed the young abstainers styling themselves the "League of Temperance," twice—once in Edinburgh, and again in Glasgow. There were over 4,000 children assembled in the Free Presbyterian Assembly-room, where I saw a sight, which, when I could look into the future, I could say from my heart, "When these shall become the representatives in the world forty years from now, should they continue to abstain, old Alcohol will die from starvation for the want of victims, and this land, long polluted, will be seen by angels with envious eyes! O, let it come!" I heard these children sing, and while they sang their parents could look with a smile as they thought of the bright future. I tried to say something, but my heart was too much disturbed. But I will tell you what I did and said after the lecture was over. I told the children there were a great many thousands of young teetotallers in America. I asked the children to give three cheers for the young abstinence cause in Europe; they did, boys and girls waving caps, pocket-handkerchiefs, aprons, &c., with a sound like that of many waters! And then "once more, three hearty cheers for all young abstainers in North America." Then it was I heard a cheer which lasted for more than a minute. The immense building in every part was crammed.

I addressed also a meeting in a large chapel in Glasgow, and that, too, was crowdingly attended,—though it is perilous for me to go to Scotland, on account of the kindness of the people. I am going again in the course of two weeks, and after enjoying several more meetings, I hope to leave *for my native land.*

O, how dear is my land to me!
If now no other way could I see
Than to swim across over the wide sea,
I'd see my home—and then see thee!

I attended at the "London Tavern" the first of a series of temperance meetings which are to be held during the coming winter, or during the World's Fair.

I cannot chronicle every event which transpired in my stay in this city. The meetings I attended in the suburbs of the city were interesting. Norwood, Kentish-town, Maberly, Westminster, &c.

Here I became acquainted with a gentleman by the name of John Cassell, a coffee-dealer, a Yankee-Englishman, tall and well made. He related to me the time when he used to deliver temperance lectures throughout the country. I believe he is now very rich. He is the principal mover in this great temperance demonstration.

My lectures and addresses were always well attended.

Here also I became acquainted with the great English Temperance Apostle Jabez Burns, D.D. Preached for him and attended several temperance lectures with him. I found him very favorably disposed to the Americans in general, and yet hates the institution of slavery.

I had to get myself an office at the Strand where I could see the people who called on me every day.

The great temperance demonstration has taken place in Drury-lane Theatre, being the largest hall or house which could be got, as the Old Exeter Hall is now undergoing repairs.

Committee after committee has called to get me to deliver addresses for benevolent purposes. Letters are pouring in from the surrounding country,—of pressing invitations. I wish I could go and see them all, it would gratify me very much.

It has been raining for some time, and the fog of this country is different from any other—the mud and fog are the same, for in these narrow streets the mud flies, and the fog is all down in the mud, so heavy is the atmosphere.

I was pleasantly quartered with a gentleman in Vincent Square while I stayed there.

This is the last Sabbath I am to be in the city.

My appointments run to the North as follows :—

Nov.	7,	1850	. . .	London.
"	8,	"	. . .	Manchester.
"	9,	"	. . .	Manchester.
"	10,	"	(Sunday,)	London.
"	11,	"	. . .	Huddersfield.
"	12,	"	. . .	Manchester.
"	13,	"	. . .	Huddersfield.
"	14,	"	. . .	York, (7 1-2 o'clock.)
"	15,	"	. . .	Darlington, (7 1-2 o'clock.)
"	16,	"	. . .	" " "
"	17,	"	(Sunday,)	Newcastle-upon-Tyne.
"	18,	"	. . .	Sunderland.
"	19,	"	. . .	York.
"	20,	"	. . .	Sunderland.
"	21,	"	. . .	Darlington.
"	22,	"	. . .	Newcastle-upon-Tyne.

Nov. 23,	1850	. . .	Edinburgh.
" 24,	"	(Sunday,)	Edinburgh.
" 25,	"	. . .	Edinburgh.
" 26,	"	. . .	Edinburgh.
" 27,	"	. . .	Dundee.
" 28,	"	. . .	Perth.
" 29,	"	. . .	Dundee.
" 30,	"	. . .	Glasgow.
Dec. 1,	"	(Sunday,)	Paisley.
" 2,	"	. . .	Glasgow.
" 3,	"	. . .	Perth.
" 4,	"	. . .	Edinburgh.
" 5,	"	. . .	Edinburgh.
" 6,	"	. . .	Travel to Liverpool.
" 7,	"	. . .	To sail for America by the steamer Africa.

Such are my appointments before I sail for my native land.

To begin with, I am not well and have already disappointed two of my audiences at Manchester. A cold has been on me which has prostrated me.

I am just able to go and fill my London appointment at the Rev. S. Luke's.

The following is the address which I gave because many here had heard of a plan which I had proposed to the general Government of this country for the purpose of doing something good for our Indians. And I delivered this for the purpose of doing the cause of my race some good before the British public.

THE EVANGELIZATION OF THE NORTH AMERICAN INDIANS.

"My people are destroyed for lack of knowledge."—HOSEA iv. 6.

"I have taken upon myself this afternoon to adopt the language of God in the mouth of His prophet, 785 years before the birth of the Saviour; and perhaps, in the midst of this crowded audience, there is no one who is more fit to adopt these words than myself. '*My* people are destroyed for lack of knowledge.'

In speaking of the history of my brethren, the North American Indians, I cannot help referring to the many evils which have tended to reduce, or demoralize, and to ruin them, since the discovery of the western continent. In view of all that I have seen, as well as of all which history relates, I can adopt the language of the text: 'My people are destroyed for lack of knowledge.' And, in speaking this afternoon briefly upon the subject, I would first endeavor to engage your attention, by referring to the means of the destruction of the North American Indians, arising from their social disarrangement—the condition in which they were found, when America was first discovered. It has been the idea of many, that the downfall and ruin of some nations is absolutely necessary, before they can be blessed by Christian education; but, on referring to the structure of society, and the elements which have caused their downfall and ruin, you will find that it has not been altogether through the iron will of Him that lives above, that they have declined and disappeared from the face of the earth. And this, which applies especially to the Indians, will be found to hold good, in most instances, with regard to the other nations of the earth. What, then, has caused the ruin and the downfall of the Indians of North America?

One of the first reasons is, that of the 273 Indian tribes of America, about a quarter of them, that have had to do with Europeans, have come in contact with the *worst classes of society*. There is a class of men, romantic in their ideas, adventurous in their spirits, and reckless in their lives, having no morals, nor fear of God's law, nor regard to the common law of mankind; and these are the first to come in contact with the different races of men all over the earth. They have nothing in the shape of morality, or of Christian education—that education which, in coming in contact with the nations of the earth, warms up their universal characteristic, which is *veneration.* These have been the men, that have sowed discord and perpetuated so many jars in our country, and produced the greatest prejudices against civilization or education in the minds of the Indians. They reason thus. If these are the specimens of civilized life, they have little predilection to become civilized after the same manner. They have little or nothing to do with Christian, civilized, good people ; they are acquainted only with the worst classes of society, who prowl about the forest, like roaring lions, and on their way sow destruction and discord ; and instead of him who once could send up a shout, and a merry shout of his children, to the skies, grief, misery and distress have, step by step, followed the course of the Indian.

The second reason that I give, why the Indians of North America have not improved, but have been reduced in numbers, since they have come in contact with European races, is, *the introduction of ammunition of war*, in the shape of rifles and muskets. It is true that the Indians were just as expert with the bow and arrow, before they came in contact with the races of men that had what they termed the "serpent, that spits out fire and death," which was their definition of a gun; but they soon saw that a shot would do more execution than an arrow; and therefore, in their wars among themselves, they have destroyed one another ten times more than before they possessed such a weapon.

The third reason is, that the Indians have been brought together on both sides of the armies of the *European powers that have fought in our country.* The Spanish, the French, the Dutch, the Americans, and the British, have all called out the aid of the savage from the forest wilds, to arm against their supposed enemies. Before this the Indians knew not what they were at war with each other for; but the Indian's prowess, bravery, stern nature, have been appealed to, and he has been caused to leave his forest wild, and in the midst of the war-shout and the death-song he has sung and danced like a fiend, intoxicated, as it were, by the promises that have been given to him, in the event of victory. But the Indian goes back to the wood, and no one cares for him, much less to teach him Christianity.

The fourth reason is, because the institutions, or at

least the *schools, that have been established in our country, have not met the wants of the Indian youth.* It has been an idea of some of our missionaries, that in order to become educated we must be taught in our own language. Therefore the Indians, in learning their own language, have perpetuated their own ideas, and had nothing to do with English literature. Twelve years ago, when I first began to speak the English language, I used to tell the missionaries—" Teach the Indian children the English language, and you will not be under the necessity of teaching them their own, for that will come to them naturally." For instance. There are some letters in the English alphabet which we omit entirely—such as *f, l, r, v, x;* these are altogether silent—we have no use for them. Now, if we are taught in our own language, we cannot make any use of these ; but the sooner we are taught the English language, the sooner will we be introduced into the wide fields of the past, as well as the literature of the white man ; and by reading, learning, transforming gradually the entire feelings, the thoughts, the actions, the very emotions of the Indian, we become even as the noble white man that loves his God. But because we have been taught in our own language, we have been perpetuating our old ideas from one to another. Two or three years back I visited the western country, went through the valleys of the Mississippi and the Missouri. There I saw that the missionaries had begun to adopt what I told them, and what they ought to have done in the first instance. Now we are twenty-five or thirty years in our progress behind what we should have been, if, at the moment we came in contact with good men, we had been taught English education. The ignorance that arises from our not learning the English language in the first instance, has been another of the means, indirectly, of the decrease of our race.

Fifthly, diseases of a *foreign nature have been introduced*—diseases which were not before known among us—such as the small-pox and other epidemics, and the diseases arising from a course of vicious habits; and nation after nation has died, through not knowing how to check these diseases. Thus, the Mandans, and others in the west, were once powerful nations. In the years '37 and '38 the small-pox raged among the nations of the west; and one of those tribes that suffered most I saw a year ago, last October. When the old chief perceived that his village was dying away every hour—that his wife was declining, that some of his family had already died, and that himself was about to fall a victim to the horrible disease, he said to his two sons—"Go to the east, to the wigwams of the white man ; never look back ; go right to the east, and tell them that we have all died here in our village." They started, and went across the Council Bluffs ; and at the fall of that year the younger of the two got his brother to go back again ; and there they saw their once populous village all desolate, and their whole country, as it were, laid waste by this dreadful disease ; and when they went to their wigwam, they saw the remains of their relatives. They hunted round the different places, to see if they could discover any traces of their father. They went just below the spring, and there they saw something in the shape of a coat ; they went up to it, and perceived the remains of their father ; his old pipe, that he often had with him in his council, lay by, his pouch also by his side. There he lay, with his head towards the water, as if he had gone there to die. The youngest of the brothers went to the top of the hill, near the banks of the river, and stood looking about wildly over the whole country, that seemed to have been covered by the ravages of disease. His brother was just in the act of going away from him; and this young man could not bear the idea that they two were the only representatives of a village of nearly two thousand people. He looked round on the country in which he once lived, and the fields over which he had sported, and seemed as if taken by despair. He seized his gun, put the muzzle of it to his mouth; and when his brother turned to look at him, he saw the flash; and he fell a victim to despair. Such are the effects of disease in our country.

The last reason that I will give, why the Indians of North America have decreased so much, is *the use of alcoholic drinks*. The Indian has no polished society to check him, no social ties to restrain him; and therefore, when he comes in contact with the intoxicating liquor he drinks and drinks, and step by step digs his grave, and down he goes. This is perhaps one of the strongest reasons I have named. The whole of our country was blessed with the smiles of the Great Spirit, before such things were introduced among us; and now what is the consequence? The gradual diminishing of some nations, and the utter extinction of others. Gradually do they recede towards the setting sun, till it has become a creed to the white man, that it is of no use to endeavor to check their progress, and to save the North American Indians.

These are some of the things, my friends, that have produced the downfall and ruin of my brethren. But I am surprised to find even in Christian lands, where I see, and am delighted to see, the white man engaged in reading this blessed Book, that he should think he discovers in that Book some things that might be construed into the idea, that the *iron law of God* is that which has crushed and made few the noble sons of America. It is not so, my brethren. I read in a different light from this the character of the God whom you love and serve. His benevolence is written in the page of nature around me; and every blade of glass, and the sweet sounds that vibrate on my ear, and salute my heart with feelings of warm emotion, tell me that the God who made the earth is a God of love. The God that we adore, my brethren, is not the author of the downfall and ruin of the North American Indians; it is the laws of nature disarranged altogether in the Indian, by the elements of destruction which I have named, which has caused his downfall.

'But,' it may be asked, 'why is it that the Indians of North America have not improved, when they have been in contact with Christian men, and since efforts have been put forth to save them?' It is too often the case, that because we place so much value on what little we bestow for the cause of Almighty God that we expect in a short time to receive an equivalent, in the shape of trophies to His glory. I have in my hand a little work, which illustrates the gradual progress of the North American Indians in literature. Among the Indians to which I belong, the Ojibway nation, our publications amount to fifty-three, consisting of translations of different books for schools, as well as the Word of God. We have a good deal of the Old Testament translated into our language, and the whole of the New Testament. The Mohawks have five or six translations of various works; the Senecas also have different translations. The Shawnees have a variety of literature, which belong to them alone. The Ottawas have five or six translations of English literature, as well as of the Bible and Testament. The Menomenes, Wyandott, Sioux, Chickasaws, Choctaws, Creeks, Osages, and the Cherokees—all these Indian nations have various books, for the purpose of improving the young mind. The Cherokees, perhaps, have improved a great deal faster than the other Indian nations, though their having been driven from their abode, the side of the Mississippi, has prevented them from improving so fast as they would otherwise have done. The Ojibways are beginning to have several of their own seminaries amongst them, for the purpose of perpetuating pure principles in our country: and if living in brick houses, and having farm-yards, that are filled with different kinds of domestic animals, and fields that wave before the wind, are no signs of civilization, the Indians will never become civilized. If the Indian, having been taught the means of elevation, have not exhibited any energy of character, in order to grasp the great truths that were presented to his mind, and store them in his heart—then his condition is a hopeless one. We have sometimes been told that the Indians cannot improve; but send one of our young men into your halls of education, and see if he will be behind four or five white boys that are sent there at the same time, with the same advantages for instruction. Not one of these I have known that have been sent into religious schools, but what has come back at least with a great deal of credit to himself, and much gratification to the hearts of those that sent him. The composition of the Indian's mind is like that of the Saxon race; it only requires hard rubbing, in order to bring out the brightest and best qualities.

'What, then, have missions done?' This has often been asked me, by people in this country, as well as in America; laughing at the idea of our missions, as if they had not done anything, and pointing with the finger of scorn at the scenes of their labors. Now, if these people can give us a plan that has worked better than ours, I certainly will adopt it, provided it be attached to the eternal throne; but do not tell me that splendid laws, and education, and such policy as this, is alone to be the means of profiting the nation to which I belong. It is not your farms nor your palaces that we want; it is that sanctified education that has made your people become powerful, energetic, and prosperous. But do not tell me that education alone is necessary, in order to elevate the Indian. Why, my brethren, I like education very well; but apart from Christianity, apart from the morals of the Gospel, it is like building a splendid mansion by the sea-side; in a few years it will begin to reel, and down it must thunder at last upon the waters. But place the edifice upon the Rock that was given for the salvation of the world, and build it as high as the skies, and it will remain, to guide the pathway of generations in the future. When you have the principles of the Gospel to cement a structure of this kind, it must stand, and perpetuate its blessings to those who live around its base. This is the kind of education that we want for the red man of the west.

We have had diversity of missions. Our Methodist friends work their way; our Presbyterian friends their way; our Baptist friends their way, the Episcopalian church their way, the Moravians their way. Why, my dear friends, when it concerns the salvation of a nation—why do we go to perpetuate the heart-burnings gendered in the breasts of those who alike read and learn the laws of God and the Word of God? If any one comes into our country as a missionary, I would to God that he would leave all his dogmas behind him, and bring the simple Word of truth in his hands, with his heart swelling with the work that is before him. It is then that he will become like a comet, blazing forth in the dark mind of the Indian. This diversity has been one of the great means of retarding the progress of improvement; because the missionaries think that they are hired, for £50, or £60, or £80 a-year, to go and perpetuate the particular views of the denomination that sent them; whereas the Indians do not even know that there are such views. We want the morals of the Gospel; we want that kind of instruction which shall open heaven itself, and let down the gentle stream of God's grace, and which, instead of diffusing discord and contending elements, shall bind society, as it were, in one, and teach men, for mutual good, to labor side by side, in unfolding the banner of Christ.

And now in reference to the cause which I have to advocate before you. Ever since the first settlement in North America, emigration has been pressing westward to the setting sun. For the last 350 years the avarice of the wicked white man has pawed and gnawed the property of the Indian, and has been crying every day, 'more land, more land;' and the Indian's wigwam has been destroyed, and he has felt the effects of the rapid stride of emigration; and this has kept him from improving, as he ought, from the missionaries. I have aided several denominations of missionaries in the west, and pointed out to them what I thought the best stations; but after laboring thus for several years, I began to see, that in order to do good we must get the Indians into a particular locality, where we might concentrate ourselves, to give them instruction of a moral and religious character. My idea has therefore been, to influence the Congress of the United States to give to us, at the north-west, a territory—a country about 150 miles square, on which to locate the Indians who are already partly civilized,—those that want to become civilized might come in one after another voluntarily,—and to let all the rest of the continent be given for the white man. If a fifth or a sixth of the proceeds of our lands, or the annuities of the Indians, were to be placed at the disposal of men capable of marking out the best places to build school-houses and provide masters, it would be sufficient for the whole country to be blessed by Christian education. Our missionaries, when they come in contact with the government, do not say anything; if they do, they are represented as being antagonistic, and the cause of both the missionary and the Indian suffer. Now let that land be given us—institutions of learning and buildings, would soon commence—to carry on a civil form of government, that the civilized Indians might, after a while, assemble to make laws for themselves; till they have irrigated the whole of that country with streams of literature and knowledge, and taken such a course as shall more endear them to the people who live around them.

I need not ask you, my friends, to listen to me as to the practicability of this design, because I have already detained you too long; but permit me, in conclusion, to say, that this state of things is desired not only by those who, like myself, have seen the necessity of such measures, but even by the Indians that know not one letter of the alphabet; and many of them have been the foremost to shake me with their warm hands, and encourage me in my visits among them, and also in claiming the attention of the American people to the subject. I remember that, in the month of October, when I went to the great Missouri river one morning, I rode about sixteen miles before the run rose, in order to see the cliffs of barren clay on the Council Bluffs. About seven miles distant the smoke from the wigwams of a thousand lodges ascended at the other side of the stream. At five miles yonder I saw the ascending of another column of smoke to the skies. When I went there, I saw an old chief. Through the medium of an interpreter—for I do not understand all the Indian languages—he asked me what I was doing in that country, since he understood I had come a great way from the north-east. He was told that I had travelled, and visited the Indian nations beyond the two valleys of the Mississippi and the Missouri, and the base of the Rocky Mountains, for the purpose of receiving their encouragement, or obtaining their assent to my plan for asking the government of the United States for a country of the description I have named. When I felt the warm grasp of this old man, nearly seventy years of age, who had seldom received the hand of a civilized Indian before, and saw the fiery spark flash from his dark eyes, of intense interest and anxiety, it was to tell me—"Onward, then, onward! Stop not at those things which may intervene. The day will come, when the Indian with the white man shall be blessed with a home like this." Yes, my brethren, difficulties have been in my way. The language I had to learn first; and I have not at command as much means as I should like. This has been another thing that has impeded my way. But if labor is to bring the object, if toil is to bring it, if energy is to bring it, I have long laid my soul and body upon the altar, for the salvation of my brethren; and I look forward to the day, when I shall see them enjoying Christian institutions, as you enjoy them. I have sometimes gone to the summit of some of your public buildings, as well as of those in other countries which I have visited, and I have seen chapels and churches rising all through the country, dotting the entire land of the pale-face ; and wherever I have seen a religious institution, it has told me that it was intended to perpetuate the glorious principles of Christianity.

When I go back to America, I hope to renew my request to the Congress. On the 25th of last February I placed a memorial in their hands ; and it has been referred to a committee. The committee have not yet acted on the measure, in consequence of the agitation on the slavery question. I expect now to go across the great deep to my native land again, to renew my request for a grant of land, there to plant missionaries, to open schools, and to invite my Indian brethren to receive education. And oh ! my brethren, shall I ask you this afternoon, that you will follow me to the setting sun with your prayers ? I have seen tears moisten the face of the white man ; I have seen his eyes swimming in the waters of sympathy ; I am glad that Providence pointed out a way for me to come to your country ; and could I but carry with me, without injury to your people, the elements which have made you become a great nation—could I but go to the west, and there sow the seed that shall spring up under the smiles of the Great Spirit, for me to enjoy a morsel of the effects of my labors, I should be richly rewarded, even though they prove not entirely successful before I die. On the 7th of December I expect to sail for America, and to call out two of my elder brethren, one to the western, another to the eastern states; and it is my purpose to go to the south, and hold public meetings all over the country, in order to bring about that kind of influence which may act upon Congress, upon a certain day, in the city of Washington On the last occasion I was asked to present my address to the two houses. I did not consent, because I had not then matured my plans so much as I have since; but if that privilege is given me, I purpose laying my plan before them, on the 25th of February, 1851, and to ask as a Christian that we may receive a grant of land, on which to plant the standard of the cross, and that as it waves there our Indian children may receive the glorious principles of the Christian religion.

My brethren, when I hear such agitation in the public

mind, with respect to the aggression of one part of what is called Christendom, in this country, I do not wish to disparage one of you by saying, that we have been sleeping for a long time, while the enemy has been watching us, and has sent his own children, even into the forests of America, and they, with their imposing pictures of saints, have set aside the heathenish worship of the Indians, and placed theirs in its stead : not a kind of Christian moral training, but only a training of the senses, instead of that heart-training which is so necessary. I do not wish for anything of this kind in my native land. I have seen these men place the cross of Christ on the tops of their churches, instead of keeping that cross in the heart, where it may be cherished, and throw out the graces that it bestows. My brethren, we want you to become our teachers. We want you to point out to us the true elements of greatness; and if we can reach your world easier, we will perhaps come and see you oftener. I am glad that it belongs to the Christians in North America, at the end of the nineteenth century, to show what Christianity has done for the Indian. I have sometimes looked at your little children that you love and admire, and as I have watched their tiny hands and feet, I have thought to myself—'Perhaps these little creatures will one day, when I am an old man, come and plant themselves in my native land; and they may be the very ones that shall lead the Indian to his God, and make the wide territory of the Indian resound with the praises of the Most High.' Send them to us, my brethren. We will cherish them near us. Oh! that God may direct their footsteps to us, that we may receive from their lips the education for which we plead for our Indians. May God prosper the white man of this country! May He bestow His mercies upon him still; and while the prayers of your children ascend from the earth, may a drop of its answer come to the wigwam of the Indian, that he may receive benefits by your gifts, by your benevolence and by your prayers!"

The above is from the British Pulpit.

On my way throughout those towns which I have visited I have found friends. And I could here fill page after page in narrative to their many kindnesses, which when I think of them I am with them. There are the friends in Darlington, Mr. John Harris, the Peeses, the mayor of Sunderland, and the mayor of Newcastle. In all the towns I have visited I have delivered lectures on subjects which are more familiar to me, such as

The Religious Belief, Poetry and Eloquence of the N. A. Indians.

The Peculiarities of the Indians—Their Manners and Customs.

The Probable Origin of the Indians and their Traditions, Courtship, &c.

One which has interested most is the following :

America : its Elements of Greatness and its Scenery.

Here is a notice of one of those from the Yorkshireman, in York :—

" A lecture was delivered on Wednesday evening, in the Lecture Hall, Goodramgate, by Kah-ge-ga-gah-bowh. Mr. Thomas Monkhouse was called upon to preside. The lecture embraced a view of America—its elements, and its scenery. The country of which he intended to speak was North America proper. The scenery of North America was one of diversified grandeur—possessing the natural features of climate peculiar to all nations—from the warmth of the south to the coldness of the north,—possessing a wildness and a brilliancy that can only be seen in the vast magnificence and variety of

America. As America was on the day when first discovered, so is she to be found at the present day. He should scorn that man who did not love his native country, and therefore he hoped his audience would excuse him. The land he was about to speak of—to place before their mind's eye, was a scene ancient in itself, sublime in its development, and one that any man might covet. In the ambrosial south was to be found everything that the heart of man could desire. He did not speak of North America as the country of his adoption. It was America, in her forests and her plains that he called his home,—it was that land which his fathers held by right and by possession. He reminded his audience that North America is washed on one side by the waves of the Pacific, and on the other by the waters of the Atlantic—on each side, therefore, bounded by two mighty oceans. Its mountains stretch far out from the south and extend away to the north, displaying the many beauties with which one half the country is interspersed, and which but few other lands could boast of. Its lofty mountains and extensive valleys possess a majestic wildness, contrasted with its universal hills. Its rivers are mighty oceans, and away into the far interior of that country, run those mighty oceans. As for its lakes they were like inland seas. The chain of lakes was connected with the St. Lawrence, and on they rolled, until, step by step, step by step, they fall down into the falls of Niagara ; and still rolling on until they emerge into the far oceans of the east. The lakes of this magnificent and fertile land were not like the little pond—but extending into the country, to the distance of two, three, four, and five hundred miles, and about 250 miles wide. In Speaking of the rivers of America the Chief related an anecdote. He was standing on Blackfriars Bridge with a friend one day, who asked him 'if he had ever seen such a river ?' 'Perhaps he had,' replied the Chief. 'I suppose,' said the friend, 'the Mississippi is a little larger ?' The Chief replied to this, 'It is a little larger, and perhaps a little clearer, too.' Speaking of the Mississippi he said, you may stand on the highest peak in the north and watch it running towards the east into the northern lakes. There sloping its course travels the Mississippi 2,500 miles until it reaches the regions of the arctic world. He came now to describe the source of this mighty river. He travelled with a friend in 1844 along this river in a canoe. After travelling through the lakes for two days and a half, they came to a place where, from the shallowness of the creek, they were obliged to lift out their vessel. Following this course for another seven miles they came to a place where they saw it bubbling forth from the side of a hill. There he laid his hands across the stream. It seemed not to move, so gentle was that tide. Then he took away his hand, and the Mississippi travelled on as usual. So small was that stream that he stepped over it and then back again, and there, lost in wonder, he stood beside that little tiny stream, and watched it pass him by ; not a noise it made. He followed the stream—that tiny thing which he held in the palm of his hand—until he beheld it deepen its way, and swell its sides, and gather a mighty power in its road. He saw it struggling, and as they turned towards the sun, they could see the mighty Mississippi rolling on its majestic course—on towards the southern climes—until it unbosomed itself in the great gulf of the south. The lecturer next noticed the snowy mountains, and others covered with fire, and having described these in his usual eloquent style, he proceeded to notice the soils of America. The soil in that land in its temperate clime is good, and he thought it the best, perhaps, for Europeans.

Whilst speaking of the soils, he deemed it necessary to make this remark with respect to emigration. Emigrants inquired as to the best places, and he advised no emigrant to go south of the southern base of the Missouri, nor north of Lake Superior, which he called the temperate climate. South of the Missouri the inhabitants are subject to bilious complaints and other diseases. The climate he pointed out was well suited to Europeans, being situate between the extreme heat and the extreme cold. With respect to the soil, he said he had observed it to be as good 5, 6, and 7 feet down as at the surface. He said a man with £1,000 could obtain one of the best farms in the western world. Having said this much for its soil, the Chief proceeded to speak of its forests in connection with its prairies. In the forests of his native land he had travelled month after month without finding an opening. It seemed a world of forest amid those lofty American pines, towering away to the height of 250 feet, —in their majesty waving and bowing in the skies— and seeming to laugh at and defy the powers of the elements. It was here his forefathers lived when first discovered. Having no fireworks to amuse themselves or their children with, sometimes the natives set fire to these forests, and then it seemed as though the whole forest world was in a blaze, throwing its lurid flame around, and lighting up the distant hills in the dead of night. The whole of this country is flat, abounding with buffalos, elks, and deer. The minerals of America were next touched upon. Abundance of lead is found in the north part of Illinois and Wisconsin. The Indians discovered this mineral about 200 years ago, and made use of it. It then lay upon the surface of the hills, and the natives used it to write thereon their traditionary stories. In Wisconsin, there is abundance of copper, as well as in the State of New Jersey. Lake Superior, also, was said to be nearly lined with copper. The Pittsburg company had made immense sums with the copper mines, and had declared a dividend of 75 per cent. The next mineral, so much coveted by the pale-face, the red-face, or the Indian as well, was gold. He exhorted his hearers to believe about one third of the stories they had heard respecting California. He next proceeded to review America as a land of promise. It was a land mighty in its natural productions. It was the residence of a race of men having mind, and lofty moral faculties ;—a nation of progress, developing the grand powers of man. When they came to view a country like this, they asked themselves, was it a country suited to the purpose of raising the man of tall intellect, of broad benevolence?—man that would take as it were the earth and put it in his heart? America was nearly a temperance country compared with ours. This was one of the elements of its greatness. It was temperance that lifted, as it were, the great curtain of ignorance from before the eyes cf the people, the sun poured in his rays of light from the skies, man rejoiced and received the benefits thereof. (Applause.) It was intemperance that had fettered and retarded the progress of Christianity in the earth. It was this evil that fettered the progress of the truths of a Luther, a Calvin, a Wesley and a Whitefield. (Applause.) It was the bottle that checked its course, and dammed its influence. They might boast of their splendid edifices, and of the diversified architecture, but as long as this demon was allowed a place in the edifice, so long would he throw his dark tail around, and sting to the very vitals! So long as this continued, so long would progress move on in its slow-coach style. (Applause.) America was a bible country; and thirdly, the Americans were a people of enterprise. After dwelling at considerable length on the scenery of America, in which he introduced and depicted in a finely poetic strain the falls of Niagara, with its boiling torrents and furious, rolling rapids, he sketched with exciting vigor the dark, deep, and rapid rivers, overhung by the perpendicular granite rock, looking down upon the current below. It seemed as though nature in some of her convulsions had split those mighty rocks in twain to make a passage for the streams. His description of a thunder-storm was sublimely grand. The Chief brought his lecture to a close by referring again to the cultivation of the soil as necessary to the existence of man, and concluded by a beautiful contrast between the wants of the body and those of the mind. At the close of the lecture an individual in the body of the hall asked the Chief as to the best period of the year for emigration to America, to which he replied that the latter end of the summer, or the autumn, was the most suitable. Before the audience separated, the Chief sang one of his native songs, in which was exhibited a good knowledge of music. The air was in a minor key, and almost consequently of a melancholy nature."

I am now in Edinburgh, just arrived from Newcastle. I am still unwell, and I am expected to deliver a temperance sermon by the Scottish Presbyterian Church Society. I have so far received nothing but kindness. O may my friends in this and other countries be ever blessed.

CHAPTER XXIII.

SCOTLAND.

I HAVE had no time to write down all the events of my interesting sojourn in this most interesting country, since I came here, for my time has been so well occupied. Now I am about to leave it, and the people who have been so kind to me.

" The metropolis of Scotland is situated in the northern part of the County of Mid-Lothian, and is about two miles distant from the Firth of Forth.* Its length and breadth are nearly equal, measuring about two miles in either direction. In panoramic splendor, its site is generally admitted to be unequalled by any capital in Europe, and the prospect from the elevated points of the city and neighborhood is of a singular beauty and grandeur. The noble estuary of the Forth, expanding

* The precise geographical position of the centre of the city is 55° 57′ 20″ north latitude, and 3° 10′ 30″ west longitude.

from River into Ocean; the solitary grandeur of Arthur's Seat; the varied park and woodland scenery which enrich the southward prospect; the pastoral acclivities of the neighboring Pentland Hills, and the more shadowy splendors of the Lammermoors, the Ochils, and the Grampians, form some of the features of a landscape combining, in one vast expanse, the richest elements of the beautiful and the sublime."

In Edinburgh there are warm hearts to be found for me and my race, though the character of the people is cold at first; but the longer I have known them has proved that they are not cold altogether.

Long time ago I read the history of these people, and particularly the Highlanders, and my predilections for this people before no doubt has had to do with the present visit.

The Edinburgh Castle is a saucy-looking place. Old fashioned fortifications and embankment rude. Houses of the ancient order. There I saw a room very small where Queen Mary lived, and where king James was born.

The most interesting to visitors now is the crown and sceptre which for years have been lost, and now they are before the gaze of this people. Made of gold. A man is stationed over or near it all the while to guard it and show it to strangers.

Looking down from the castle the sight is most charming. The panoramic view of the Forth before you and sails which everywhere dot over the whole surface of the water—the country and towns—the farms and the surrounding hills all in grand array. And in the midst of this wild scenery, there, from that hill you can see the column of granite erected to the memory of Sir W. Scott, and that of Burns, Nelson, and King George the Fourth.

The old part of this city is an antique place, and away below it is the "Holyrood Palace." On the left is the new Hospital, and before you is the Royal Academy of fine arts. Church after church is in sight.

The hill on the east of this is a very good place to view from. The names of Mr. John Dunlap, Dr. Gunn, the Rev. Wm. Reid, Johnson, and my devoted and affectionate A. Young, A. Harmour, and not forgetting my dear friend and brother P. Sinclair and family. May Heaven still smile on them.

My visit to Dundee was on many accounts the pleasantest. In delivering my lectures before the people I had the Independent Church, and George Duncan, M. P.

presided at the first and the next time, one of the officers of the town. A very interesting event for myself, inasmuch as I think the people were gratified and looked as though they were happy. The Rev. gentlemen of this city all attended my lecture. I became acquainted here with one Mr. J. Valentine, and his name is a guarantee that he is a charming man. Dundee is a well-located place, on the side of the Dee facing the sun. The surrounding country looks as though no other people could live here but the Scotch people.

In the summer it must be a lovely place.

While I was there I visted the celebrated astronomer, Dr. Dick, who lives in Broughton Ferry, four miles below Dundee, in a beautiful location facing the mouth of the river, and surrounding hills. It was after dark when we entered his house, and found telescopes pointing to every window, small and great. And in his studio lay sheets of paper and one of these half written on. His books all arrayed around the room in a perfectly *liter*ary style.

His person is a middle-sized man, leans forward—and not fleshy, face sharp, and a well-developed forehead, begins to walk rather infirm. He seems to be so happy. Speak of America, his heart is full of gratitude to his friends in New York, Philadelphia, and in different parts of the country. He said he should like to visit the New World if it was not for the voyage, and there he is tied and his wife, so devotedly attached to him, that she has to say where he should and where he should not go. As we sat at tea I found myself contemplating the days of my school-hours, when I read his books with avidity. Now, here he is. This is the man who has travelled with the circuit of the sun, and wandered in the realms of the stars, collecting new beauties and new glories from the grandest objects of heaven.

It is he who led me, my bewildered mind lost in the magnitude of thought, that a God who made the worlds to sing his praise was a God of Power.

When I asked him of his circumstances he replied, "I have enough, for the time I may live." And may he always have.

Perth is another well-situated town at the river Dee. I had a meeting here and gave an address to about 3,000 people in the City Hall. That is, it will seat that number—but the crowd was so great I think there could not have been less than 500 more, for it was literally crowded.

I met some of the society of Friends here, and found them well informed about America. The lord Provost presided, the next time I visited Perth. I went up the highest hill and viewed the country. Below us was the river Dee, and before us were hills which began to assume a sackcloth-like appearance, and the frost on the hills made their brows look gray. Then at some distance a railroad car flew past in an opening plain, and went in one side of the hill and came out whizzing on the other side, *red-hot*, for it was nearly dark, and the streak of fire was singularly conspicuous.

My Dr. Valentine, I shall often think of this place after this.

All that I have seen of this country is delightful indeed. The hills along towards the Highlands are remarkable—few trees on them; yet clothed with an underwood where grouse is hunted after the 12th of August.

My visits to Glasgow and Paisley were very interesting to me. On the Sabbath, the 1st of December, after a fatigued labor of the past week, I had to speak in the Parish Church to over 3,000 souls on the subject of Temperance. On Saturday before, to a large audience in Glasgow.

I stayed in Paisley with one Dr. Richmond, and just by is the oldest ruins of the place. The chapel where the Monks and Jesuits used to live when they had their day of glory and power. A very curious building it is too. It was raining when I went around to see it. Wrote my name, and sung a song in the "echo chamber." I visited no one but a Mr Kerr, a shawl manufacturer, and from him I received good expression of sympathy for the good of my people. I went to a poor dilapidated hut near the falls of this stream which rolls down in steps just by. And here the Dr. informed me of the fact that yon college-hut was the birth-place of Wilson the state ornithologist of New York.

It is related in his biography that he expressed a wish, when conversing upon the subject of death, that when he died, he might be buried where the birds should come and sing over his grave. And these sentiments are also ours.

THE LAST WISH.

" In the wild forest shade,
Under some spreading oak, or waving pine,
Or old elm, festooned with the gadding vine,
Let me be laid.

In this dim lonely grot,
No foot intrusive, will disturb my dust,
But o'er me, songs of the wild bird shall burst,
Cheering the spot.

Not amid charnel stones,
Or coffins dark, or thick with ancient mould,
With lattered pall, and fringe of cankered gold,
May rest my bones;
But let the dewy rose,
The snow-drop and the violet lend perfume,
Above the spot, where in my grassy tomb,
I take repose.

Year after year
Within the silver birch-tree o'er me hung,
The chirping wren shall rear her callow young;
And the red robin, the green bough among,
Shall build her dwelling near;
And ever at the purple dawning of the day,
The lark shall chant a pealing song above,
And the shrill quail, when eve grows dim and gray,
Shall pipe her hymn of love.

The black-bird and the thrush,
And golden oriole, shall flit around,
And waken with a mellow gush of sound,
The forests' solemn hush.
Birds, from the distant sea,
Shall sometimes thither flock on snowy wing
And soar above my dust in airy rings,
Singing a dirge to me!"

On Monday morning I left for Glasgow, where I delivered my last lecture before the Temperance society, at the Rev. Dr. Robinson's Church. The weather being very unfavorable, there was not much of an audience. Glasgow is more like the American cities in point of business, and the busy commerce which everywhere is visible.

Tuesday again I was in Perth, when the lord Provost presided over my meeting, and again cordially received.

For the last time and place I was in Edinburgh, Wednesday and Thursday. Thursday evening there was a tea party, which was tendered to me by the ladies of Glasgow at the Queen St. Hall. And there for the last time I addressed with a heart too full, a people who had won my best affections. Speeches were made by Dr. Gunn, Rev. W. Reid, Mr. Dunlap and others. I could have enjoyed the meeting if it had not been that it was the last meeting.

I bid a final affectionate farewell to my friends. Archibald Young, who had given me the ink-stand which I have used constantly since, and other things for my wife and son. May heaven bless the dear boy of his, never will I forget his kindness. Now while I am here in the New World I can see how he appeared when

I last saw him. Peter Sinclair and family, they shall have a warm corner of my aching heart. I hope to see them again. Friday morning, 6th Dec., the morning was clear and the air bracing. I left for Liverpool. After a ride of six hours I was then seated in the Waterloo Hotel.

Saturday morning, 7th Dec. I went on board the fine new steamer "Africa." The same gallant Captain Ryrie, with whom I came over from America, was then the Captain, and was about to leave again.

I might say a great deal about the sea or the storms which I experienced in coming over; but, I would just say for the consolation of those who are obliged to go over and are as often sea-sick as I was: "*that a man is a fool who sails from Liverpool in the month of December.*"

I have seen the storm in the lakes of the west, and in the wild woods when trees lay down to die, the sweeping tornado uprooting the trees, when I have felt the very earth trembling on account of fallen trees. But this storm and gale in a sea is most terrific and awful.

The waves knocked the bell from its iron frame, tore

up the side-bulwarks, shattered the figure-head, and awfully scared some of our ladies.

On the second Sabbath morning out I heard by the sailors we had now met a gale, and that we did hardly make three miles in an hour—the waves soused, and thumped the ship, and the waves would roll over the deck, and rush front and aft, and the noise it would make in the dark was awful. At this stage of affairs I said to myself that I should crawl out of my berth and dress myself to see the storm. I creeped up to the deck, and the ship rolling on her sides plunging her paddle-boxes into the water, and then again bouncing up and then again down, the sea all in a foam! the rigging of the ship moaning and whistling. Just as I was getting up the quarter-deck a sea struck the bow of the ship, and then the water arose and in one grand sheet fell lengthwise on the deck, and falling on me, which nearly struck me from my hold. Perfectly drenched, salt in my mouth and my eyes, snorting with it, I dabbled down to my berth, perfectly willing to go down to the bottom any time after that, and sick—sick—ah! yes—I was sick indeed.

The sea in the time of a gale is the grandest sight

that my eyes ever beheld. Our noble steamer seems at times a lion, and battled the giant waves, and at times motionless would appear, trembling, stunned by the fury of the waves.

I am now safely housed in the Irving House, and three nights I have spent on my couch, and each night I have awoke myself in giving my bedstead, a deadly grasp, as I did to my berth while I was on the ocean.

I am now again in America, and thank the Great Spirit for it. My friends are here, and how they came all around me. The many questions I have been asked about the Old World, how I liked it, and what I saw, and to satisfy them I have given a short outline of my journey.

I hope to go again and see the far East, and if possible to seek the footprints of the Saviour, who, as it is said, came to earth to bless man. A land made memorable by the acts of Him who gave the best laws for the government of man.

I add here a welcome from a friend of mine in the city of " Brotherly Love."

TO GEORGE COPWAY, OF THE OJIBWAY NATION.

" Hail to thee, chief, from the far forest land !
Hail to thee, prince, of the wild wood-land !
From the sun-crowned hills of the glorious west,
Where wild winds billow Superior's breast,
Thou hast travelled o'er broad Atlantic's foam,
Where sages of peace to their councils come ;
Thou hast trodden in halls of ancient glory
And traced the records of olden story ;—
Thou hast seen grim relics of ruthless ire,
And tortures unknown at thy camping fire.
The war-fiend was worshipped by pale-faced men,
As well as by braves in the forest glen ;
And torrents of heart-warm, human blood
Have poured over Europe, as wasting flood.
But the worship and honor of carnage is past,
Earth's glorious jubilee soundeth at last ;
Child of the forest ! to thee it is given
To speak in rich cadence the message of heaven ;
And bid the paleface with the Indian combine
The oak of our country with olive to twine ;
To bid the wild war-notes forever be still,
While angels are chanting, " On earth good will,
And glory to God in the highest above,
The Father of all, the fountain of love."

PHILADELPHIA. A. W. H.

J. C. RIKER,

PUBLISHER AND BOOKSELLER,

129 FULTON-STREET, NEW-YORK,

HAS RECENTLY ISSUED THE FOLLOWING

NEW WORKS AND NEW EDITIONS.

THE GOVERNESS; or the Education of Circumstances. 12mo., cloth. 75 cts.

"One person is more, and another less, the creature of circumstances, but no one is altogether independent of them."

KATHERINE DOUGLASS; or, Principle Developed. By S. Selby Coppard. 12mo., clo. 75 cts.

"This story is a domestic one, and charmingly written."

AMY HARRINGTON; or, a Sister's Love. By the author of the Curate of Linwood, etc. 12mo., clo. 75 cents.

"If other love wound, this falleth soft
On the tired heart, like evening dew;
In life and in death, in sorrow and joy,
A sister's love ever is true."

THE LIFE OF SILAS TALBOT, Commodore in the United States Navy. By Henry T. Tuckerman. 18mo., cloth. 38 cts.

"Mr. Tuckerman has rendered an excellent service to our historical literature, by the publication of this pleasant and well written volume."

THE ITALIAN SKETCH BOOK. By Henry T. Tuckerman. 12mo., cloth. $1.

"This is a new edition of a beautiful and popular work, written with all the author's grace and richness of style and clearness of thought and description."—*Boston Courier.*

THE EMPEROR JULIAN and His Generation. By Dr. Neander. 12mo., clo. 75 cts.

"It takes in the entire range of the history of the Christian Church as well as the personal history of the Emperor."—*Commercial Advertiser.*

J. C. RIKER,

HAS IN PRESS AND WILL SHORTLY PUBLISH:

STUDIES AND STORIES, from Chronicle and History. By Mrs. Hall and Mrs. Forster. Freely Illustrated.

HERBERT TRACY; or the Trials of Mercantile Life and the Morality of Trade. By "A Counting-House Man." Designed for Young Men.